Trafficking Hadassah

The representation of sexual trafficking in the book of Esther has parallels with the cultural memories, histories, and materialized pain of African(a) girls and women across time and space, from the Persian Empire, to subsequent slave trade routes and beyond.

Trafficking Hadassah illuminates that Africana female bodies have been and continue to be colonized and sexualized, exploited for profit and pleasure, causing adverse physical, mental, sexual, socio-cultural, and spiritual consequences for the girls and women concerned. It focuses on sexual trafficking both in the biblical book of Esther and during the transatlantic slave trade to demonstrate how gender and racism intersect with other forms of oppression, including legal oppression, which results in the sexual trafficking of African(a) females. It examines both the conditions and mechanisms by which the trafficking of the virgin girls (who are collectively identified) are legitimated and normalized in the book of Esther, alongside contemporary histories of Africana females. This important book examines ideologies and stereotypes that are used to justify the abuse in both contexts, challenges the complicity of biblical readers and interpreters in violence against girls and women, and illustrates how attention to the nameless, faceless African girls in the text is impacted by the #MeToo and #SayHerName social movements.

This book will be of particular interest to those studying the Bible, religion, gender, theology, and sex trafficking. It is also an important book for those in the related fields of Africana Studies, Trauma Studies, Post-Colonial Studies, Diaspora Studies, Critical Race Studies, as well as to the general reader.

Ericka Shawndricka Dunbar is Visiting Professor of Hebrew Bible, Payne Theological Seminary, Wilberforce, Ohio, USA.

Rape Culture, Religion and the Bible

Series Editors: *Caroline Blyth, University of Auckland, New Zealand*
Johanna Stiebert, *University of Leeds, UK*

For more information about this series, please visit: www.routledge.
com/Rape-Culture-Religion-and-the-Bible/book-series/RCRB

Trafficking Hadassah

Collective Trauma, Cultural Memory, and Identity in the Book of Esther and in the African Diaspora

Ericka Shawndricka Dunbar

Routledge
Taylor & Francis Group

LONDON AND NEW YORK

First published 2022
by Routledge
2 Park Square, Milton Park, Abingdon, Oxon OX14 4RN

and by Routledge
605 Third Avenue, New York, NY 10158

Routledge is an imprint of the Taylor & Francis Group, an informa business

British Library Cataloguing-in-Publication Data
A catalogue record for this book is available from the British Library

Library of Congress Cataloging-in-Publication Data
Names: Dunbar, Ericka Shawndricka, author.
Title: Trafficking Hadassah : collective trauma, cultural memory, and identity in the Book of Esther and in the African diaspora / Ericka Shawndricka Dunbar.
Description: Abingdon, Oxon ; New York, NY : Routledge, 2022. | Series: Rape culture, religion and the Bible | Includes bibliographical references and index. |
Identifiers: LCCN 2021038517 | ISBN 9780367769116 (hbk) | ISBN 9781003168911 (ebk)
Subjects: LCSH: Human trafficking—History. | Women, Black—History. | Body image—History. | Bible. Esther. | Group identity. | Collective memory.
Classification: LCC HQ281 .D84 2022 | DDC 364.15/51—dc23
LC record available at https://lccn.loc.gov/2021038517

ISBN: 978-0-367-76911-6 (hbk)
ISBN: 978-0-367-76912-3 (pbk)
ISBN: 978-1-003-16891-1 (ebk)

DOI: 10.4324/9781003168911

Typeset in Times New Roman
by codeMantra

Contents

Acknowledgments

I wish to express my sincerest gratitude to Drs. Johanna Stiebert, Katie Edwards, and Caroline Blyth and to The Shiloh Project for your endless support. Thank you for creating opportunities to both engage and collaborate in activism that resists gender-based sexualized violence and, to present my scholarship, especially as a contributor to the Routledge-focused series.

Dr. Randall C. Bailey: You are my inspiration and accountability partner for this work.

Much appreciation to my mentors at Drew University for your perceptiveness and support throughout the writing and editing of this project: Drs. Kenneth Ngwa, Traci West, Angella Son, and to Dr. Danna Fewell.

To my family: my husband, Johnathan Hill; grandmother, Doris Pitts; parents, Jacqueline Hart and Vedrick Dunbar Sr; siblings, nieces and nephews, and closest friends. Thank you for giving me life and the DNA of resilient survivors! I appreciate your prayers and support. Dr. Uylee R. Waugh, you'll always be the light of my life. Thanks for illuminating the journey with your transcending presence. This book is dedicated to your memory.

To my other mentors and colleagues: Dr. Carolyn McCrary, Dr. Jesse Mann, Dr. Tat-Siong Benny Liew, Dr. Patrick Reyes, Dr. Marlene Ferraras, Graham Stetler, Donna Matteis, Irma Sanders, Dr. Beverly Wallace, Dr. Kimberly Russaw, Dr. Shively Smith, Dr. Nami Kim, Dr. Rosetta Ross, Dr. Janet Wolf, my FTE and CDF families, Bishop Teresa Jefferson-Snorton and Bishop Marvin Frank Thomas Sr., and the Christian Methodist Episcopal Church. Thank you for investing in me and giving me the opportunities to use the gifts that God has blessed me with.

An Introduction to reading Esther 1–2 as a Story of Sexual Trafficking

This book focuses on sexual trafficking both in the biblical book of Esther and during the transatlantic slave trade. Methodologically, I employ Africana biblical criticism as the means to place the particularities of Africana[1] life, history, and culture at the center of the interpretative process. I investigate and describe sexual trafficking in both literary and cultural/historical contexts to illustrate that sexual trafficking is a collective, communal issue that disproportionately impacts minority and minoritized groups. Further, my project demonstrates how gender and racism intersect with other forms of oppression, including legal oppression, which results in the sexual trafficking of minoritized groups. I argue that sexual trafficking constitutes cultural trauma that marks the identity and memories not only of individuals but also of collectives in often damaging and irrevocable ways. Thus, this project elucidates the relationship between collective trauma, identity, and memory.[2] Drawing on the theories of intersectionality, collective memory, collective trauma, and horror, my reading of Esther contributes to and expands the #SayHerName movement, calling attention to global instances of violent abuse against Africana females. I focus on Esther because the book's location in the Persian empire is characterized by socio-cultural practices and ideologies that normalize and minimize the sexual trafficking and abuse of countless individuals in the story world. The story specifically refers to the geographical locale of Ethiopia, signifying that African girls are among those trafficked to the king's palace. I give careful attention to ideologies and stereotypes used to justify such abuse, the conditions and mechanisms by which the virgin girls in the story are trafficked, and the traumatic impacts of sexual trafficking on individual and group identities.

Moreover, this book offers a dialogical reading of the book of Esther with histories of Africana females of the transatlantic slave

DOI: 10.4324/9781003168911-1

trade. As such, it discusses the cultural trauma of sex trafficking among African(a) girls and women across contexts (ancient-biblical and contemporary) – including examination of the US slave trade and its reverberations right up to the twenty-first century. As a dialogical cultural study, this project contributes to and expands Esther studies by shedding light on the ancient community's struggle to deal with sexual violence and exploitation. At the same time, it sensitizes contemporary audiences to the wider social and global problem of sexual trafficking. My intersectional analysis offers a new direction in Esther discourse, revealing the systematic establishment and mechanisms of sexual trafficking in the book of Esther, including identification of the parties involved. Further, it illumines the complexity, fluidity, and diversity of diasporic identity marked by contestation and negotiation in colonial contexts. The two aims of this book are: first, to challenge the complicity of biblical readers and interpreters in violence against girls and women; and second, to illustrate how attention to the nameless, faceless African girls in the text is impacted by social movements such as #MeToo and #SayHerName.

I structure the book as follows: In this Introduction, I will define sexual trafficking and discuss the scope and range of this global phenomenon. I also outline the theoretical and methodological approaches that frame my dialogical cultural study. In Chapter 1, I then apply these definitions of sexual trafficking to the first two chapters of the book of Esther and engage with sexual trafficking discourse to make visible the manifestation and mechanisms of sexual trafficking in the narrative. To summarize, the two opening chapters of the book of Esther detail gender-based violence (GBV), sexual exploitation, and horror. I draw particularly on the second chapter of Esther, where the king's imperial court – in consultation with the royal servants – conceptualizes and implements the following policy:

> Let beautiful young virgins be sought out for the king. And let the king appoint commissioners in all the provinces of his kingdom to gather all the beautiful young virgins to the harem in the citadel of Susa under custody of Hegai, the king's eunuch, who is in charge of the women; let their cosmetic treatments be given them. And let the girl who pleases the king be queen instead of Vashti.
>
> (Esther 2:2b–4a NRSV)

As explained in Chapter 1, sexual exploitation commences in Esther 1 with Vashti and intensifies in Chapter 2 when virgin girls are captured and transported for this purpose across national geographical boundaries to the king's palace in Susa. After displacement from their homes and provinces, the virgin girls are shuffled from one harem, to the king's bedroom, to another harem, as their bodies become object/abject for the king's sexual pleasure. The king and his officials, who represent Persian colonial powers, orchestrate and implement a sexual trafficking system, whereby virgin girls are brought from all over Ahasuerus's empire for his sexual consumption and gratification. Sexual trafficking is therefore embedded within the narrative, and the movement of sexually trafficked girls includes, notably, racialized, minoritized bodies.

Chapter 2 delineates instances of sexual trafficking during the transatlantic slave trade and centers these as a site of collective memory for Africana girls and women. Both Jewish and African diasporic identities emerge in contexts marked by colonialism, capture, sexual exploitation, displacement, genocide, ethnic suppression, and the need for cultural persistence in such horrific and hostile environments. My investigation assesses the conditions and processes by which female collectives are trafficked in the contemporary context and, the traumatic impact of trafficking on collective identity and memory. In addition, I discuss the centrality of movement and boundaries in sex-trafficking enterprises.

Chapter 3 analyzes stereotypes and socio-cultural attitudes regarding Africana female sexuality. Attention is given to euphemisms and cover-ups in the sacred text, and to attitudes and practices in contemporary contexts that further contribute to and exacerbate sexualized violence and rape culture. In addition, because Esther 1–2 describes gendered violence, horrific exploitation, and there is other widespread gruesome violence throughout the book, I suggest the book of Esther should be considered as belonging to the genre of biblical horror. I elucidate how the application of the humor/comedy genre can instead direct readers away from those elements of the text, such as sex trafficking, that are too often ignored in traditional Esther discourse. In doing so, readers/interpreters continue, if inadvertently, to cover up or mask the sexualized abuse and ignore or fail to critique rape cultures. Other iterations of horror, beyond the traumatic sexual encounter, include additional physical, psychological, biological, and spiritual impacts on both individuals and collectives, as well as challenges to researching sexual trafficking.

The concluding chapter summarizes the main arguments put forth in the book and outlines the implications of my hermeneutical orientation, both for biblical studies and the #SayHerName movement. My intersectional polyvocal framework opens up the text in different and meaningful ways that enable readers and interpreters to acknowledge and address social and cultural complexities that arise from living in societies marked by kyriarchy, colonialism, and patriarchy. Specifically, my interpretation allows readers and interpreters to recognize various types of systematic and structural violence perpetrated against African(a) females and geographical locales in ancient and contemporary contexts, to critique these intersecting forms of violence, and to consider the role that sacred stories play in creating and maintaining hierarchies of power, alongside their impact on the psyches and identities of readers.

Sex(ual) trafficking defined

Sexual trafficking is a multifaceted, complex phenomenon that is growing in scope and magnitude and presents a threat to already vulnerable and marginalized persons globally. Specifically, the trafficking of women and children has become an urgent concern for nations around the world. Sexual trafficking is one of many forms of human trafficking and, economically speaking, one of the most profitable. Recognized as an organized crime, sexual trafficking is "the recruitment, transportation, transfer, harbor, or receipt of people, by coercive or abusive means for the purpose of sexual exploitation" (US Department of State Trafficking in Persons Report). It takes the forms of forced sexual slavery and sex work, forced marriage and child marriage, child prostitution, and/or forced pornography, including of children (Davis and Snyman 2005). Sexual trafficking is associated with and recognized as a form of GBV. GBV includes physical, sexual, and psychological violence inflicted upon individuals or collectives on account of gendered norms and unequal power distributions (United Nations High Commissioner for Refugees).

Three elements of trafficking

There are three elements of trafficking: the process, the means, and the goal. The process involves recruitment, transportation, harboring, transferring, and/or receiving. The means are through threat, force, fraud, coercion, abduction, deceit, or deception. The goal is sexual exploitation, prostitution, pornography, slavery, forced labor, debt bondage, and/or involuntary servitude: all physically embodied outcomes. Economic mobility is also a goal of human and sexual trafficking. According to the US Department of State, only one element must be present in order to constitute trafficking ("Human Trafficking

Defined," US Department of State Diplomacy in Action). If the goal is sexual violence or exploitation in any form, sexual trafficking is at issue. Consent, or the lack thereof, is not sufficient for identifying victims of sexual trafficking, because consent, as mentioned, is often obscured by other situations of vulnerability, including but not limited to gender discrimination, oppression and violence, forced displacement, poverty, war, and lack of options and opportunities.

Parties involved in sexual trafficking

Sex trafficking typically involves four key parties: the perpetrator, the vendor, the facilitator, and the victim. The perpetrator sexually exploits the victim. The vendor extends the services and capital, making sexual trafficking possible. The facilitator expedites the victimization process. Finally, the victim is the one who is sexually exploited (Beyer 2001: 308). These elements and parties involved bringing focus to my investigation of the virgin girls in the narrative world of Esther and of Africana girls and women during the transatlantic slave trade, firmly identifying both as victims of sex trafficking. Furthermore, the interconnections between the two disparate examples show that sexual trafficking is a fixture of empire building and an urgent category of study (among other forms of extraction and abuse) in postcolonial and empire studies.

Sexual trafficking is a geopolitical issue but one that lacks a comprehensive framework for understanding and evaluating the structural and cultural factors that create and support its manifestations. Operated as an underground enterprise, sexual trafficking thrives on silence, invisibility, and the heightened vulnerability of victims. Reporting is further complicated by the dynamic and unpredictable nature of global events and by a lack in uniformity of reporting structures. The International Labor Organization reports that in 2016, at any given time, 40.3 million people were in modern slavery and that one in four victims of modern slavery were children. Moreover, women and girls are excessively affected by forced labor accounting for 99% of victims in the commercial sex industry and 58% in other sectors (Global Estimates of Modern Slavery: Forced Labour and Forced Marriage Report). According to the Polaris Project which focuses on the US context, reports of trafficking increase yearly but trafficking remains underreported. This also reflects global trends.

Although unable to provide a full picture of the scope of trafficking, the Polaris Project notes that the majority of persons who are trafficked are from vulnerable populations such as oppressed or marginal groups, the poor, and undocumented migrants, groups that are often disproportionately represented by minority and minoritized people of color. Their 2016 statistics report reveals that, of the 7,572 cases reported to their trafficking hotline, 77% were sexual trafficking or sex and labor-related trafficking cases. Of the 8,542 survivors, 7,128 were female. Of the 3,116 survivors that reported their race/ethnicity, 2447 were Latino/a, Asian, African, African-American, Black, and multi-ethnic/multi-racial (2016 US National Human Trafficking Hotline Statistics, Polaris). Even with tremendous underreporting, this gives us a small snippet of the scope and scale of global sexual trafficking and its impact on minoritized children and women. Similarly, and more recently, the US Department of State released a 2020 *Trafficking in Persons Report* that is based on information gathered from 148 countries. This report reflects the trends of the Polaris Project report: that the most common form of global human trafficking is sexual trafficking (77% among women; 72% among girls) and victims predominantly girls and women (roughly 70% of all victims) (*Trafficking in Persons Report 20th Edition*, US Department of State, January 2021).

The United Nations Convention on Transnational Crime Article 3a further delineates that human trafficking is:

> The recruitment, transportation, transfer, harboring or receipt of persons, by means of threat or use of force or other forms of coercion, of abduction, of fraud or deception, of the abuse of power or of a position of vulnerability or of the giving or receiving of payments or benefits to achieve the *consent* of a person … for the purpose of exploitation. Exploitation shall include, at minimum, the exploitation of prostitution or other forms of sexual exploitation, forced labor or services, slavery or practices similar to slavery, servitude or the removal of organs.
>
> (UN Convention against Transnational Organized Crime and the Protocols Thereto, italics added)

There are many issues with the concept and role of consent in definitions of sexual trafficking, including with determining if and when someone, especially a child, can grant consent. Other challenges posed are that consent is often dubious, because it is obtained through improper, coercive, or deceitful means, or because consent at any one stage does not provide consent for all stages of the process of trafficking. In some situations, girls and women consent because they believe they have no other or no better options ("The Issue of Consent"

Toolkit to Combat Trafficking). These challenges highlight the ambi-guity in notions of consent and the complex and problematic nature of sex trafficking. British lawyer Helena Kennedy adds that consent within legal frameworks is based on a sliding scale proportionate to gender, ethnicity, race, class, and economic worth (Kennedy 2005). Additionally, stereotyping and vilification of minority ethnic girls and women often undermine both their credibility and their consent.

Social conflict, displacement, little if any legal ramification for sex-ual exploitation, globalization, forced and non-forced migration, do-mestication,[3] patriarchal culture, and racist stereotypes all exacerbate the problem of sexual trafficking and increase victims' vulnerability. Although current understandings and manifestations of globalization are not congruent with representations of globalism in the book of Esther, empires of antiquity functioned as mini globalizers, involv-ing political, economic, and cultural forces that had enduring effects on civilizations and colonized cultures. Empires are contributors to waves of globalism as they impose social institutions and engage in networks of trade. This is depicted in the book of Esther when the king imposes political, economic, and cultural institutions throughout his empire that fans out from Susa, the empire's center, as far as Africa and India. The account also reflects unequal power distributions among the provinces, enabling the king to capture female virgin girls in the colonized regions under his rule. In addition, empires, through local technologies, participate in the transformation, dissemination, and globalization of knowledge production – such as, in Esther, through decrees and edicts, which dispersed ideologies far and wide in ancient communities. When the king utilizes decrees to capture girls for his sexual pleasure, he, by legalizing his action, promotes the perception and legitimacy of ethnic, colonized virgin girls as sexually exploitable. And this is then dispersed to all the peoples throughout his empire.

Patriarchal culture further adds to women and girls' susceptibility to sexual exploitation. Natividad Chong, for instance, cites domestic-ity and the social isolation it fosters as especially detrimental. This is because of the expectation in traditional patriarchal cultures that women exhibit obedience, submission, silence, and lack of resistance. In such cultures, women are more likely to refrain from seeking help or refuge from abuse in both domestic and sex trafficking environ-ments. Furthermore, in patriarchal cultures, recourse to justice is a privilege afforded primarily to men, to preserve the well-being and in-terests of males. These cultures, therefore, contribute to females being prevented or stifled in their efforts to denounce abuse and trafficking (Chong 2014: 208).

Migration is also intimately connected to sex trafficking. Numerous victims voluntarily migrate, looking for new opportunities, while others are unwillingly uprooted. Important to note, migration results from conditions similar to those that allow sexual trafficking to thrive such as poverty, discrimination, lack of opportunity, violence, and family breakdown. These conditions contribute to victims' increased vulnerability to and lack of protection from sexual trafficking. What further ties these contributing factors together is a global colonialist culture that affords men the power and authority to define gender norms and boundaries, along with the power to force movement and migration, and the authority to transgress bodily boundaries of females without penalty.

Criminologist Caitlin Jade van Niekerk maintains that feminist approaches to trafficking allow for the establishment and necessity of "gender" as a critical category of analysis, which she claims other psychological and social theories do not allow (2018: 17–27). She writes, "feminist-abolitionist discourse argues that the trafficking of women is a violation of human rights, thereby suggesting that sexual exploitation is a manifestation of men's power over women, violating their physical integrity and subordinating their sexuality" (2018: 18). It is, however, necessary to recognize that females also exercise abusive power over other females, violating a subordinate female's body and sexuality. This is evident in the many instances where white women appropriate and exploit the bodies, sexual and labor powers of Africana girls and women, such as during and following the transatlantic slave trade, to maintain colonial culture, to please their husbands, and in order to feed, nurture, and teach their children. These experiences have resonance with what the biblical character Hagar experiences at the hand of Sarai (Gen. 16). Black feminist and womanist scholars contend that a framework of intersectionality is key to analyzing systematic and systemic oppression because it illuminates the inextricability of gender, race, and class and the asymmetrical sexual relationships between colonizers and Africana females that have been foundational to colonizing cultures. The application of intersectionality also enables readers and interpreters to see how Africana girls and women are often made invisible and marginal, and their sexuality sometimes pathologized in these blatantly gendered and politicized spaces.[4]

The global pervasiveness of sex trafficking and the complex damage it inflicts bring multiple challenges, not only for human rights groups, for nurses, and other medical and public health practitioners, and for politicians, but also for scholars across a range of disciplines. Understanding the mechanisms of trafficking, and then confronting the problem and its impact on victims, alongside addressing cultural perceptions and attitudes, and implications for economies and societies is a very daunting undertaking. It requires effort and input from multiple directions, including from religious actors.

Methodological and theoretical framing: intersectionality, polyvocal hermeneutics, and storytelling

Many biblical scholars note the role of gender in the sexual exploitation of Vashti, Esther, and the female virgins in the book of Esther.[5] However, not enough attention has been given to the role of ethnicity in contributing to their vulnerability to and experiences of sexual exploitation. Drawing on antecedent scholarship, I want to examine the intersection of ethnicity/race, gender, and class within the text, with particular focus and emphasis on sexual trafficking and its implications for the book of Esther. I argue that, and show how, the application of intersectionality and polyvocality opens the texts up, allowing interpreters to identify and explore complex elements and processes of sexual trafficking in Esther.

A critical spin must be employed in biblical hermeneutics to recognize the depiction of sexual trafficking in the book of Esther. This spin must apply intersectionality and polyvocality. Kimberlé Crenshaw cites Black women's race, gender, and class as all contributing to their disadvantage and discrimination, which, she argues, leads to harsh consequences (1989: 140). Crenshaw endorses discarding single-axis frameworks that reflect "uncritical and disturbing acceptance of dominant ways of thinking about discrimination." Such a credulous lens of analysis distorts the multidimensionality of Black women's experience. This, in turn, goes on to lead to the theoretical, methodological, and practical erasure of Black women and collapses Black women's experiences under the collective experiences of other ethnic women (1989: 139). Intersectionality, however, enhances appreciation and assessment of the "unique compoundedness of their situation and the centrality of their experiences to larger classes of women and Blacks" (1989: 150). Thus, intersectional analyses of violence allow readers and interpreters to address more adequately the particular ways that Black women are oppressed, subordinated, and discriminated against (1989: 140). It also enables readers to see markers of difference as mutually constitutive and contributing to personal and social oppression and privileges. Moreover, it will enhance our ability to see and to interpret the sexual exploitation of the virgin girls in the book of Esther as sexual trafficking.

Polyvocality, meanwhile, is a literary device that is characterized by multiple and varied voices and/or perspectives. Attention to textual polyvocality deepens, expands, and problematizes any single-axis gender analysis because it encourages diverse readings and interpretations of texts, rather than a preferred dominant interpretation. Polyvocality is also spatial and layered: it welcomes reflection on the multiple spaces summoned and controlled in a narrative, and on the multiple layers of subjugated, suppressed, and often silenced identity within an individual or within a female collective. The text of Esther describes the experiences of a diverse set of girls from varied ethnic backgrounds and geographical locations. Not only must we engage the voices and experiences of the muted, frequently overlooked, and ignored characters within the book of Esther, but polyvocality can also create the space to facilitate conversations with other biblical scholars who either missed or ignored critical elements, cues, and references in the text that identify intersectional oppressions. This literary device allows interpreters to reconsider the framing of the experiences of the virgin girls by means of a beauty pageant, and to identify it as sexual trafficking.

While gender and ethnicity are typically considered by modern interpreters when assessing the main character Hadassah (better known as Esther), hermeneutics of intersectionality and of collective trauma can enhance interpreters' understandings of how gender and ethnicity intersect with other markers of difference for other female characters in the book. This perspective considers the roles of racism, sexism, classism, and nationalism in the treatment and exploitation of Vashti and of the virgin girls in the first two chapters. The virgins' ethnicities, gender, class, and national identities coupled with silence around their abuse raise questions. Silences regarding their intersectional identities and their abuse raise more questions, including about how the book is interpreted and to what ends. What do interpreters miss and/or and ignore? What is at stake ethically in traditional interpretations of this text? What is the role of law in perpetuating abuse and injustice?

A framework of intersectionality and polyvocality sheds light also on how African girls and women continue to be rendered invisible in the reception history of Esther. By failing to address the experiences, abuse, and traumatization of the African girls in the book of Esther, interpreters (albeit often inadvertently) uphold ideologies that either African(a) girls and women cannot be violated, or that their violation is irrelevant. Intersectionality and polyvocality, on the other hand, advance our analysis and understandings of marginalized identities and social locations, as well as of the oppressive systems that exploit them.

Storytelling is another method that I employ as a critical spin in my interpretation. Storytelling is universal and thus meaningful across cultures. Thus, in this book, I treat the book of Esther as a story. When read alongside indigenous stories of the lived experiences of Africana girls and women, and alongside other stories offered by diverse scholars, these multiple and varied stories all together hold the promise of shedding fresh light on practices of meaning-making and understanding. This method of interpretation talks back to sexual trafficking and to colonizing and patriarchal societies and cultures by emphasizing the physical, social, emotional, and spiritual impact on Africana females' bodies, psyches, spirits, and identities.

Not only does storytelling offer knowledge from invested and attached participants and observers, but it challenges and calls listeners to respond and act, to raise voices of protest to the traumas represented in the stories. It challenges recipients of the stories to assess how they contribute to or how they may counter the moral and ethical challenges that are presented. In this way, there is an interactive exchange between the stories, the communities that produce them, and their recipients, all of which expand and diversify meaning- and knowledge-making. This book includes knowledge resources from peoples across disciplines. The intention of this is to encourage readers analytically and creatively to embrace new ideas and new knowledge and to take part in creating sustainable solutions to issues such as sexual trafficking, GBV, intersecting gender, racial, and class oppressions, and colonialism, among other pervasive, systemic problems.

Many scholars argue that it is anachronistic to propose that there are sexual trafficking economies in the ancient context. While I recognize and understand that the Bible was written in and for cultures distinct from modern ones, there is a trend in biblical scholarship to interpret texts with contemporary phenomena and questions in mind, to determine how these experiences and understandings shape interpretations and identities. This book in no way suggests that the ancient communities that produced the book of Esther understood or defined their practices as "sexual trafficking." Instead, it argues that definitions of sexual trafficking and sexual trafficking discourses illuminate practices depicted in the text that are analogous to what contemporary readers and interpreters understand as sexual trafficking.

I connect this interpretation with experiences of sexualized violence in histories of other Africana girls and women, in particular, with the capture, transportation across the Atlantic Ocean, and enslavement of millions of Africans in various "new" lands, exploited, plundered, and stolen by colonial forces. This historical audacity is termed the

Maafa.[6] The enslaved of the Maafa became the property of slave owners who controlled their bodies, both physically and sexually. Cultural historian David Davis notes that not only did slave owners have sexual access to slaves, but their sons and overseers coerced and raped the wives and daughters of slave families as well (Davis 2006).

Although the book of Esther is a story written and constructed centuries ago, it has resonances with the cultural traumas of contemporary African diasporic subjects at the hands of neo-imperial and neo-colonial powers. Africana bodies are both relegated and regulated for the sexual pleasure of the imperializing king and patriarch and to secure the stability of imperial and patriarchal structures. Capture, forced displacement, imperial domination, cultural genocide, ethnic suppression, eunuch-making, and sexual trafficking are experiences that invite dialogue between the two contexts. Both colonial subjugation and forced displacement result in social fragmentation of those conquered and dislocated; both make Africana bodies susceptible to violation. By reading the book of Esther through the lens of African diasporic experiences of trafficking, this book illuminates how cultural/ethnic minorities and gendered minorities experience heightened vulnerability to trafficking which, in turn, affects collective cultural trauma.

Sex trafficking statistics reveal that brown and black girls in contemporary contexts are disproportionately vulnerable to and targeted by traffickers. Similarly, in the book of Esther, the narrator reveals that the virgin girls abducted and brought to the king's harem (Chapter 2), are transported from provinces that span from India to Ethiopia (1:1). On that account, the girls in the narrative world are taken from provinces that are in our contemporary context inhabited predominantly by brown and black populations. My research undergirds claims that Africana females were, historically and intergenerationally, and continue to be, culturally victimized and traumatized by exploitative trafficking systems.

The first two chapters of the book of Esther capture and epitomize the cultural memories and histories of Africana girls and women across time, space, place, nations, oceans, and continents. Esther 2, especially, has strong resonances with the materialized pain, primping, and pimping of forcibly diasporized Africana female bodies of the slave trade. When read alongside these experiences of Africana girls and women, the words in the story of Esther are made flesh, and dwell among us, teaching us about Africana materiality, sexuality, and spirituality. It teaches us how colonization and sexualized traumatization marks the bodies, identities, memories, and histories of African diasporic peoples in very specific ways.

My multi-methodological approach to biblical interpretation is attentive to the cultural identity, politics, and economics of Africana people. It foregrounds Africa and Africana subjects in the Bible and their stories and histories that include experiences of sex trafficking. Further, it affords an interpretative space from which I identify and critique ideologies regarding Africa/Africana peoples and the gendered colonial language and imagery that is present throughout the book of Esther. One ideology that stands out in particular is the inferiorization and subjugation of Africana peoples, who are dehumanized, their identities destabilized, thereby justifying their oppression and exploitation. In addition, by reading the Bible alongside other texts, I can interrogate and challenge how the Bible has been used to perpetuate violence and to grant validation for colonialism, sexual terrorism, and symbolic and physical abuse. Intertextual analyses will take the form of Africana hermeneutics as storytelling.[7] That is, I will situate myself as the storyteller in dialogue with scholarship within the broader fields of biblical studies, psychology, and ethics, in an attempt to propose reading methods that make meaning and justice at the interface of the biblical text and the history of Africana girls' and women's lives.

This hermeneutical framing takes on particular significance in light of the traction and momentum of the #MeToo movement, which in recent years has shed new light on the sheer ubiquity of sexual abuse and exploitation. The movement is a timely response to enduring issues of GBV, sexual exploitation, and sexual trafficking. Invisibility and silence around sexual harassment, abuse, and exploitation, especially of minority and minoritized women, is what precipitated Tarana Burke to initiate the movement.[8] Burke, who works with victims of sexual abuse, noted the debilitating trauma caused by gender-based sexualized violence as she listened to women's stories and recognized her own failure to respond. Reading the book of Esther with particular attention to and emphasis on the sexual trafficking of Africana girls highlights the longstanding ideologies, stereotypes, and actions that constitute, undergird, and perpetuate the types of abuse and sexual exploitation that the #MeToo movement challenges and resists; and it expands the theoretical and interpretative space of biblical scholarship toward liberative ends.

The #SayHerName movement, meanwhile, raises awareness of the names and stories of Africana girls and women who have been victimized by violent and racist police and to offer support to their families.[9] The African girls in the book of Esther are like many contemporary Africana girls and women, too, impacted by political, racialized, *and* sexual violence, but their names and stories are not given voice in the story world. Consequently, we cannot literally #SayHerName. We can, however, as morally and ethically responsible biblical interpreters, acknowledge and bear witness to the plight of these girls whose names we will never know. We *can* stand with those impacted by sexual violence and exploitation throughout history and up to the present day, and commit to read between the lines, behind the euphemisms, and through the silences and silencing in the biblical text and in narrated stories of Africana girls and women across time and space. In doing so, we will redeem the stories and dignity of all the girls and women whose voices have too often been silenced.

Notes

1 When I refer to Africana girls and women, I refer to the collective communities of girls and women located on the continent of Africa, and/or who descend from them, and/or who have been displaced from the continent through the transatlantic slave trade or voluntary and involuntary migration.

2 This project is not meant to minimize, judge, or further marginalize those affected by sexual trafficking. Neither do I argue that all Africana girls and women have been sexually abused, trafficked, or have limited agency. Rather, I provide evidence that colonizers targeted and trafficked African(a) girls and women in the book of Esther and particularly during the transatlantic slave trade. I provide a nuanced analysis of the contexts that render girls and women vulnerable, as sexual slaves with restricted agency and power.

   Although some readers and interpreters deem the girls and women powerless in the story world, the actions of Vashti and Esther shed some light on how people with seemingly little agency and power can engage in practices that liberate them from oppressive structures. Esther uses sex and sexuality (5:1–8) to persuade the king to allow her to approach him and speak. Though her agency and power are restricted, she negotiates within structures of subordination, patriarchy, and colonialism in ways that render her as more than an essentialized victim. It is therefore critical to be careful with how we label those affected by sexualized violence. Although many scholars use the term "victim," perhaps victim-survivor is a more useful designation for underscoring and emphasizing the agency, power, and resistance of Vashti and Esther. This will help readers avoid one-sided interpretations of girls' and women's agency and power and prevent vicarious objectification. Yet, sadly, not all victims of sexualized abuse survive. In this book, I use the terms "victim" and "abusee" interchangeably to refer to those impacted by sexual trafficking.

3 "Domestication" refers to practices of exploitation and control over a human being by another human being. See, "What is Domestic Slavery," https://www.antislavery.org/slavery-today/domestic-work-and-slavery/.

4 See Evelynn Hammonds, "Toward a Genealogy of Black Female Sexuality: The Problematic of Silence," in *Feminist Theory and the Body: A Reader* (New York: Routledge, 1999): 93–104; and Emily West and R. J. Knight, "Mothers'

Milk: Slavery, Wet Nursing, and Black and White Women in the Antebellum South," in *Journal of Southern History* Vol. 83, no. 1 (2017): 37–68.
5 See Randall C. Bailey, "That's Why They Didn't Call the Book Hadassah!": The Interse(ct)/(x)ionality of Race/Ethnicity, Gender, and Sexuality in the Book of Esther," in *They Were All Together in One Place? Toward Minority Biblical Criticism*, edited by Randall Bailey, Tat-Siong Benny Liew, and Fernando Segovia (Atlanta: Society of Biblical Literature, 2009), 227–250; Sarojini Nadar, "Gender, Power, Sexuality and Suffering Bodies in the Book of Esther: Reading the Characters of Esther and Vashti for the Purpose of Social Transformation," in *Old Testament Essays* Vol. 15, no. 1 (January 2002): 113–130; Michael V. Fox, *Character and Ideology in the Book of Esther.* Second Edition (Grand Rapids: William B. Eerdmans Publishing Company, 1991); Nicole Duran, "Who Wants to Marry a Persian King? Gender Games and Wars and the Book of Esther," in *Pregnant Passion: Gender, Sex, and Violence in the Bible*, edited by Cheryl A. Kirk-Duggan (Leiden: Brill, 2004), 71–85; Danna Nolan Fewell, "Nice Girls Do," in *The Children of Israel: Reading the Bible for the Sake of Our Children* (Nashville: Abingdon Press, 2003), 133–195.
6 Maafa is a term coined by Marimba Ani, to represent the history, genocide, and enduring effects of slavery and anti-Black racism and discrimination in the African diaspora. The term is an appropriation of the Swahili word meaning "disaster or catastrophe." It has resonance with *Shoah,* which denotes the Jewish Holocaust. See Dona M. Richards, *Let the Circle Be Unbroken: The Implications of African Spirituality in the Diaspora* (Trenton: Red Sea Press, 1994).
7 See Funlola Olojede, "Storytelling as an Indigenous Resource in the Interpretation of Old Testament Ethics and Religion," in *Scriptura* Vol. 113 (2014): 1–9.
8 See Tarana Burke, "#Metoo Was Started for Black and Brown Women and Girls. They're Still Being Ignored," *The Washington Post,* November 9, 2017; Cristela Guerra, "Where Did 'MeToo' Come from? Activist Tarana Burke, Long Before Hashtags," *Boston Globe*, October 17, 2017.
9 For further details, see the official #SayHerName website, accessed October 31, 2019, http://aapf.org/shn-campaign.

Works Cited

Beyer, Nancy. "The Sex Tourism Industry Spreads to Costa Rica and Honduras: Are These Countries Doing Enough to Protect Their Children from Sexual Exploitation." *Georgia Journal of International & Comparative Law* 29 (2001): 301–333.

Chong, Natividad Gutierrez. "Human Trafficking and Sex Industry: Does Ethnicity and Race Matter?" *Journal of Intercultural Studies* 35, no. 2 (2014): 196–213.

Crenshaw, Kimberlé. "Demarginalizing the Intersection of Race and Sex: A Black Feminist Critique of Antidiscrimination Doctrine, Feminist Theory and Antiracist Politics." *University of Chicago Legal Forum* 140 (1989): 139–167.

Davis, David B. *Inhuman Bondage: The Rise and Fall of Slavery in the New World 1882*. New York: Oxford University Press, 2006.

Davis, Linda and Rika Snyman. *Victimology in South Africa*. Pretoria: Van Schiak, 2005.

"Global Estimates of Modern Slavery: Forced Labour and Forced Marriage Report." September 19, 2017. Accessed, October 20, 2019, https://www.ilo.org/global/topics/forced-labour/lang--en/index.htm'.

Kennedy, Helena. *Eve Was Framed*. London: Random House, 2005.

Polaris. "2016 US National Human Trafficking Hotline Statistics." Accessed October 20, 2019, https://polarisproject.org/wp-content/uploads/2019/09/2016-Statistics.pdf

United Nations. "The Issue of Consent." *Toolkit to Combat Trafficking*. Accessed April 20, 2020, https://www.unodc.org/documents/human-trafficking/Toolkit-files/08-58296_tool_1-3.pdf.

United Nations High Commissioner for Refugees. "Sexual and Gender Based Violence." United Nations High Commissioner for Refugees. 2017. Accessed April 4, 2020, https://www.unhcr.org/en-us/sexual-and-gender-based-violence.html.

United Nations Office on Drugs and Crime. *UN Convention against Transnational Organized Crime and the Protocols Thereto*. (New York: United Nations Publications, 2004), Accessed March 18, 2020, https://www.unodc.org/documents/middleeastandnorthafrica/organised-crime/UNITED_NATIONS_CONVENTION_AGAINST_TRANSNATIONAL_ORGANIZED_CRIME_AND_THE_PROTOCOLS_THERETO.pdf

US Department of State. *Trafficking in Persons Report 2014* (Washington, DC: US Department of State Publications, 2014), Accessed December 29, 2019, http://www.state.gov/j/tip/rls/tiprpt/2014/index.htm.

US Department of State. *Trafficking in Persons Report 20th Edition* (Washington, DC: US Department of State Publications, January 2021), Accessed July 14, 2021, https://www.state.gov/wp-content/uploads/2020/06/2020-TIP-Report-Complete-062420-FINAL.pdf

van Niekerk, Caitlin Jade. "Interrogating Sex Trafficking Discourses Using a Feminist Approach." *Agenda* 32, no. 2 (2018): 17–27.

1 "One Night with the King"

Sexual trafficking in the book of Esther

In this chapter, I outline sexual trafficking as I see it depicted in the book of Esther. I argue that sexual exploitation begins in Esther 1 when Vashti is summoned to endure the sexualized gaze of the king and his inebriated male peers. Further, I point out that Vashti's punishment for refusal to acquiesce is connected to and results in a legalized sexual trafficking enterprise that is facilitated in the second chapter. I identify the process, means, and goals, as well as the parties involved in sex trafficking economies. I then analyze themes and terminologies central to trafficking, such as beauty/beautification, law, circuits, hotspots, silence, naming/namelessness, time, characteristics of traffickers, luring, and recruitment tactics among other factors that contribute to vulnerability.

A survey of literature on Esther reveals that there are diverse interpretations of the book's content, message, meanings, and implications. Since the book takes its name from one of the major characters, Esther, who becomes queen, and ultimately saves the Jews from impending genocide, many authors focus on themes such as Esther's heroine status, her agency, and use of power to cooperate with and/or resist imperial rule. Furthermore, since Mordecai assists Esther as she maneuvers through gender, ethnic, and sexual threats, many scholars focus on him, his role in preventing the imminent genocide, and his rise to the status of second-in-command to the king. Attention to gendered dynamics, which open and run throughout the book of Esther, reveals that male-female relationships are central to the plot of the book and illuminate ideologies, perceptions, and stereotypes about females in the ancient world. In addition, a schism between Mordecai and Haman and the introduction of the virgin girls in terms of their nationalities underscore that ethnicity/race and nationality inflect this gendered storyline.

DOI: 10.4324/9781003168911-2

In what follows, I will highlight some prominent themes discussed in Esther discourse to highlight features of life under colonial domination and in diaspora. In addition, I will delineate how the narrative depicts the Persian Empire constructing patriarchy and sexual trafficking. The Persian colonial setting allows the sexual exploitation of female characters. Patriarchy, male supremacy, beauty, beautification, pageantry, law, secrecy, and hiding, how time is marked, erasure, isolation, and other forms of violence, are themes deserving particular attention because they are woven throughout the first two chapters of Esther. Assessing this constellation of themes together illuminates how sexual trafficking, facilitated in the book of Esther, is situated in a broader context of colonialism, and is characterized by gender hierarchies, political conflicts, abuses of power, hostility, domination, brutal sexual and physical violence, and the need to survive amid these harmful conditions. This intersectional analysis of themes already explored by interpreters offers a new direction in Esther discourse, revealing the systematic establishment and mechanisms of, and parties involved in, sexual trafficking in the book of Esther.

An overview of sexual trafficking in the Esther 1–2

Setting the stage for trafficking: sexual exploitation in Esther 1

"Patriarchy" literally means "rule of the father" (Griffin, Dictionary of Gender Studies, 2017) and reflects the tradition of senior males ruling in all sectors of society, encompassing personal and political, private, and public spheres. Patriarchy thus reinforces sexual differentiation and privileges males over females. Privilege and supremacy of males over females are norms embedded also in the social milieu of the book of Esther. Issues of gender confront the readers from the very first chapter. In Esther 1, the narrator reveals that males and females gather at separate banquets. Furthermore, elaborate descriptions are given about the king and his male officials while briefer details are provided concerning Queen Vashti and the females at her banquet. The narrator introduces the king in grandiose terms: Ahasuerus (in some versions identified as Xerxes) rules over 127 provinces, and, in the third year of his reign, gives a banquet lasting 180 days for all his officers and ministers. The narrator provides additional details of lavishness: about army men, nobles, and governors, all of whom are males, and about the "great wealth of [Ahasuerus's] kingdom and the splendor and pomp of his majesty" (1:4). After the lengthy banquet culminates, a shorter seven-day banquet begins. All the men in Susa are present and permitted to drink without restraint. This takes place in the interior of the palace, the décor of which is amply described (1:1–8). All of these details signify hegemonic masculinity: the power to rule, control, and dominate; elaborate material possessions; and the ability to drink excessively.

By contrast, the narrator introduces Vashti in one sentence (1:9), revealing her name, status as queen, and that she hosts a banquet for the women in the king's palace. As host of her own banquet, Vashti comes across as somewhat autonomous, uncontrolled, and free.[1] Vashti lives, acts, and moves inside the king's palace where she functions as an independent person, a position that is audacious and dangerous for a female in a male-controlled space. It is therefore possible that Vashti, a gender-norms-challenging person, provokes masculine fragility, which, in turn, elicits a strong and defensive reaction to her assertion of independence and, later, resistance.

The narrator recounts that the king hosts all the men in Susa, and gives the names of the seven eunuchs, and the positions of the other males in the story world – but the narrator fails to provide any details about Vashti: her background, family, or other aspects of her identity, including her ethnicity. The lack of information functions in two ways: to narratively erase Vashti no sooner than the king legally erases her later in the narrative, and to foreshadow Vashti's fate. Two other examples of narrative erasure illuminate the narrator's commitment to patriarchy and kyriarchy.[2] First, the narrator lists the names of all the king's eunuchs and sages, while all females at Vashti's party remain nameless. Second, while multiple men are given voice, Vashti never speaks. Thus, the text constructs Vashti, like the other women in her entourage, in terms of narrative silence and erasure, which serves as a preparatory first step toward the sexual exploitation of women that follows in Chapter 2. Sexual and sexualized violence thus begins with narrative silencing and incorporates a sexualized gaze with which the females of the story become detached from the named and articulate communities. A nameless, faceless, voiceless victim – whether in the story world or our world – proves easier to exploit and to erase.

As the plot unfolds, the narrator reveals that the king commands seven eunuchs to bring Vashti before him, a command she refuses to obey. Ahasuerus summons her to show off her beauty because she is fair to behold (1:11). We learn only from the narrator that Vashti resists this sexualized gaze; her voice is not recorded (1:10–12). I want to juxtapose this with the king's official, Memucan, who does speak (1:16–20) (at some length no less!) while Vashti, the queen, remains mute throughout.

Vashti's refusal enrages the king, as is denoted by the Hebrew *chemah ba'ar,* she causes "his anger to burn within" (1:12). In response, Memucan proposes that the king issue an unalterable royal decree to banish Vashti, to depose her as queen, and to give her royal position to one "better than" her. At first read, the meaning of "better than" appears ambiguous. One may interpret that "better" indicates one more beautiful than Vashti since it is her beauty that the king desires to show off when he demands Vashti appear before his male gathering. But, since the conversation is about disobedience, we can conclude that Memucan means to give Vashti's royal position to someone who will obey the king and accept her subordinate position to men.

There are two Hebrew words used to describe Vashti: the first, *yophi,* translates as "beauty"; the second, *tov,* translated as "fair" (1:11). The latter can also mean "pleasant" or "agreeable." Therefore, Memucan is suggesting that the king replace Vashti with someone who not only looks good but will comply and not resist her husband. Beauty or good looks is not only central and contributes to the sexual exploitation of Vashti, but, as we will see in the next section of this chapter, beauty and beautification are apparatuses utilized by traffickers to facilitate and intensify abuse. Moreover, traffickers expect the abusee to conform to their desires and control without resistance. Perhaps even more important is the collective kyriarchal system of male domination. Hence, Memucan frames Vashti's refusal and agency in terms of both personal *and* political disobedience and proposes that such be punishable by law. The expectation expressed here is that females should acquiesce to the demands of the king and other males, notably husbands. This expectation is held by parties that engage in trafficking as well.

By refusing to be paraded before the drunken king and his inebriated party guests, Vashti defies and threatens the patriarchal order, kyriarchal power system, and (fragile) social stability. Consequently, she is deposed, abandoned, and degraded. A law is created and employed as a tool to assert and reassert male control and dominance over the female collective. The judicial statement, that "every man be master in his own household," is made in retaliation to Vashti's disobedience and to send a warning to other women who might be inspired by her action (1:17–18). This law is written "so that it may not be repealed" (1:9), thus sealing it into imperial legal codes in perpetuity. In addition, the king's dismissal of Vashti ultimately leads on to a situation where girls are sought, transported, held in custody, subjected to a year-long beautification process, and then sexually abused and exploited by the king (2:1–9) – all of which is depicted as necessary and legitimate.[3]

For such a time as this?: The intensification of sexual exploitation through trafficking in Esther 2

As noted in the Introduction, sexual trafficking is defined as "the recruitment, transportation, transfer, harbor, or receipt of people, by coercive or abusive means for the purpose of sexual exploitation" (US Department of State 2014). These processes are evoked within the book of Esther, although they may not always be recognized as such by the reader. Sarojini Nadar points out that, "little attention is paid to the king's selection process—the narrative quickly shifts from Vashti to Esther—and the result is erasure from our awareness that sexual violence against females occurs" (2006: 88–89).

Readers may likewise fail to see the significance of how the girls get to the king's palace in the first place. Virgin girls are abducted from their native lands, which fall under imperial rule and span from India to Ethiopia (1:1). They are transported to Persia, apparently without their agreement (2:3, 8), and are held captive in the king's harem until they receive a year of beauty treatments (2:12). After this process is over, they are taken to the king, so that he can have (non-consensual) sex with them until he determines who best satisfies him sexually (2:4, 8). These elements of abduction, transportation, and captivity are all stages in the process of sex trafficking. Recognizing this process for what it is as it unfolds within the narrative exposes the inherent violence and horror of this biblical text of terror.

How the narrator marks time or utilizes time to reveal the duration of certain traumatic encounters is another issue under-discussed by commentators of Esther. Time plays an essential role in the narrative's development. It often goes unnoticed, but, as Sarojini Nadar emphasizes, this violence takes place *over four years*. There is a *four-year lapse* between Vashti's deposition and Esther winning the king's "favor." Readers are told in 1:3 that Ahasuerus gave a banquet "in the third year of his reign," which is when Vashti is deposed and exiled. Then, in Chapter 2, Esther is taken to the king's palace in the tenth month (Tebeth) in the seventh year of his reign. We are also told that one year is spent preparing the virgins with cosmetic treatments: six months with oil of myrrh, and six months with perfumes and cosmetics (2:12). Therefore, the processes of sexual exploitation are lengthy and elaborate (2006: 87–88).

Highlighting the lapse of time underscores the longevity of the abuse and, possibly, the intensity of trauma endured. One can imagine how traumatic it might be for a child to anticipate and at the same time endure, a year-long preparation for rape and exploitation, followed by a three-year period of persistent abuse and imprisonment in multiple harems. The length of the cosmetic treatments intensifies the violation of their bodies and, possibly, leads on to suppression of identity, and to fragmentation of the mind into different parts of the traumatized self. Both experiences force the girls to adapt to colonial pressures and landscapes much like how brutalized Africana subjects were transported, dispersed in, and forced to submit or adapt to various new colonial practices and landscapes.

As mentioned in the Introduction, there are three elements of trafficking: the act/process, the way/means, and the goal. All are mentioned in the king's servants' speech (2:2–4). By imperial and patriarchal decree, virgin girls are to be sought out and transported to the king's palace: that is the act/process. Once the process is suggested by the servants and approved by the king, the tactics or means are carried out by the king's commissioners: young girls are gathered by the commissioners and brought to the king. This is a strategy of disempowerment for sexual exploitation: the goal.

Specifically, the text discloses that the officials gather many girls (*na'arot* is translated as "young women" in the NRSV, obscuring that these are children), transport them to Susa, and place them under the custody of Hegai, the king's eunuch (2:8) in preparation for sex. The virgin girls are (possibly violently) separated from their natal homes, subjected to a beautification process that includes pampering and perfuming for a year, are then shifted from one harem to the king's bedroom, to another harem, as night after night the king sexually exploits each girl in turn. After Esther is chosen to replace Vashti as queen, the girls remain: alienated, silenced, and rendered invisible – indefinitely. That these vulnerable girls are kidnapped, transplanted against their wills, and are sexually exploited by the king in his palace, all constitute sexual trafficking. Furthermore, these processes reflect a system of sexual trafficking that includes partnerships and organization, the recruitment and abduction of victims, transit, control, retention of victims, and wide-scale sexual abuse and internment.

As well as seeing the processes of sexual trafficking echoed in the opening chapters of Esther, we can also identify characters here who fulfill the four key roles typically found in trafficking: namely, the perpetrator, the vendor, the facilitator, and the victim (Beyer 2001: 208).

King Ahasuerus is the perpetrator: he sexually exploits the victim. The king's servants play the part of the vendors, who extend the services and capital that make sexual trafficking possible. The officers in the provinces of the king are the facilitators, expediting the victimization process. Finally, the victims of sexual exploitation are the many virgin girls brought to the king's harem.

The series of cities, states, nations, or continents between or among which victims of trafficking are moved is considered the "circuit" ("Trafficking Terms," Shared Hope, 2019). In the book of Esther, the circuit is established in the first two chapters. The king's vendors indicate that virgin girls are gathered by appointed commissioners in all the provinces of Ahasuerus's kingdom. The scope of his kingdom is specified in the first verse: he rules 127 provinces from India to Ethiopia, with Susa, the residence of Persian kings, as the power center. The circuit of the trafficking system and the market for the girls is, therefore, the expanse of the king's 127 provinces.[4]

Once drawn into the system, victims are transported from their homes and homelands, across boundaries within the circuit to trafficking destinations known in modern societies as "hot spots" or "brothels."[5] Hot spots are sexual encounter establishments (Farley 2006: 132). They can be houses, apartments, trailers, business facilities, etc. Within these establishments, victims have little if any control over the conditions of their lives and living situations. In the book of Esther, the hotspot is the king's palace. It is the place where the king's officials gather the virgin girls for the king's consumption and pleasure.

Recognizing these different roles within the narrative, the circuit, and identification of the king's palace in Susa as the hotspot, allows us unequivocally to identify the events as sexual trafficking. Furthermore, the trafficking is extensive: the king does not act alone but is assisted by his servants and commissioners. Their legally sanctioned collective efforts demonstrate that the sexual trafficking of beautiful young virgin girls is a highly organized institutional strategy. And yet, in the traditions of interpretation going far back, the events of Esther 1–2 are most often framed in ways that completely obscure the violence of sexual trafficking inherent in this text. In the next section, I will examine the roles of beauty, beautification, and pageantry in sex trafficking to illuminate that many traffickers take advantage of beauty and organize beautification processes and competitions to exploit the abusees' physical looks and, in contemporary settings, their hopes, and dreams.

Examining the roles of beauty, beautification, pageantry, and law in sex trafficking enterprises

In traditions of interpretation, the events of Esther 1–2 are predominantly understood as a beauty pageant, which masks sexual trafficking. For example, Michael Fox describes the king's selection process of Esther as a competition, wherein the girls are judged according to their beauty and sexual expertise. He notes that "the first stage is not a contest—the desirable girls are *simply gathered* with no regard to whether they proposed themselves for the honour or whether they were offered by their fathers" (1991: 27, italics original). While Fox acknowledges here that the girls may not have come to this contest voluntarily, he focuses instead on the *honor* that will eventually be bestowed upon the contest winner. To become Ahasuerus's new queen, he suggests, is more desirable than the alternative of "a barren life of imprisonment in the discarded concubines' seraglio" (1991: 28). Fox suggests that the *real* competition commences a year after the girls undergo cosmetic treatments when they are judged on who can best "please" (1991: 28), or, as Randall Bailey phrases it, "sex" the king (2009: 237). Fox also points out, "nothing but attractiveness to the king and sexual skills will, in this legendary account, determine who will become queen of Persia" (1991: 28).

Nicole Duran also frames the sexual exploitation of the virgin girls in terms of a competition: "Young women from far and wide come to compete for the hand of a rich and powerful man ... and the powerful man *seems to rule the proceedings* which are set up for his benefit and amusement" (2004: 71, italics original). Here, Duran ignores two descriptions in the narrative that suggest these girls do not "come to compete" voluntarily. First, the king's servants say, "Let beautiful virgin girls *be sought* out for the king. And let the king appoint commissioners in all of the provinces of his kingdom to *gather* all of the beautiful young virgins to the harem" (2:2–3, italics added for emphasis). Second, the narrator reveals that when the king's order and edict are proclaimed, many young women were "gathered" in the citadel of Susa and Esther was "taken" into the king's palace (2:8). These girls do not appear to be acting of their own volition: rather, they are repeatedly acted *upon*, being "sought," "gathered," and "taken." Duran describes the beautification process as an effort that Esther and the virgin girls make to meet the criteria for the king's beauty contest. Duran, however, does not place the beautification process under the rubric of abuse; instead, she describes beauty as a "useful" quality that the girls could deploy to survive and gain position and security.[6]

In contrast to Duran's framing, I argue that the beautification process is a tool of the king and empire to sexually exploit the girls trafficked into his palace.

Elsewhere, Duran does recognize the potential for violence in the narrative. She notes,

> the fact that sex is part of the competition and the virgins, win or lose, are no longer virgins once they have been in the competition lends Esther's story a scarier tone ... these women – more like girls – *are forced to compete,* and in a society where virginity is a girl's only ticket to respectable adulthood, the losing contestants stand a great deal to lose.
>
> (2004: 73, italics original)

She describes the gathering of the virgin girls into the king's harem as a form of kidnapping, observing that "Esther is in the court not because she wants to be but because the king is in search of an obedient wife ... she is 'gathered' (2:8) with the rest of the maidens – this is part of the king's privilege, to have his choice of the populace for his wives" (2004: 77). Sidnie White Crawford writes of the abuse,

> The contest in 2:1–4 is a sexual one, and the prize is the royal crown. The only qualifications are youth and beauty. The author doesn't comment either negatively or positively about this objectification of women, although to a modern reader it is deplorable.
>
> (2003: 692)

Youth and beauty are the selection criteria for exploitation and abuse. But the determinant for who becomes the next queen, is sexual skill – not the girl's youth or beauty.

When introduced in the story world, the virgin girls are described as *tôb*, translated twice as "beautiful" (2:2, 3). In addition, when Vashti (1:11) and Esther (2:7) are introduced, both are described as beautiful as well. Beauty is not only a physical attribute but a commodity: beauty reflects that Vashti, Esther, and the virgin girls provide visual pleasure to the males who look at them. In both ancient and contemporary contexts, beauty and beautification play a significant role in sexual trafficking. Polaris outlines that human trafficking manifests in many forms and permeates a range of industries all related to beauty ("The Typology of Modern Slavery," Polaris 2019). As such, the king's servants, like many modern-day traffickers, exploit and economically benefit from beauty and beautification.

Details of the beautification process are elaborated:

> The turn came for each girl to go in to King Ahasuerus, after being twelve months under the regulations for the women, since this was the regular period of their cosmetic treatment, six months with oil of myrrh and six months with perfumes and cosmetics for women.
>
> (2:12)

While some commentators focus on beautification techniques, several deduce that this scenario is a beauty contest in which the girls are competing to become the next queen. In so doing, they tend to fail to problematize both the girls' inability to consent and the length of the beautification process. Even more disturbing, the beauty regimens are legalized just like the trafficking and attendant violence. The narrator shows this legalization by the description, "under the regulations for the women" (2:12), with *dath* (translated here as "regulation") constituting a royal edict or statute (BDB, entry 1881).

Modern-day traffickers regularly take girls and women to beauty salons to ensure that their hair and makeup are done before sexual transactions occur. Unfortunately, women who style victims' hair and makeup are often concomitant victims of labor and sexual trafficking. Many are forced to participate in preparing other females for exploitation and sexual trafficking. Sometimes, women willingly lure, coerce, and discipline other females. One of these dynamics may be at play in the book of Esther. It is ambiguous who facilitates the perfume and cosmetic procedures. Is this beauty process facilitated for *and by* women? Whether by women or by the eunuchs, the virgin girls experience multiple offenses in the course of being trafficked.

Hebrew *tamruwq* (2:3, 9, 12) is translated as "purification" (BDB, entry 8562) or "cosmetic treatments" (NRSV). Michael Fox points out that these girls are not applying oils and perfumes (cf. 2:12) themselves but are having their bodies subjected to chemical baths (1991: 35).[7] The girls are not only forced into the king's palace, but they are not given a choice about undergoing the cosmetic treatments either. Functioning as a detergent, these bodily scrubbings ensure "purity" – which is ironic, since the girls are virgins, already embodying sexual purity. The year of preparation is, therefore, for the king's pleasure. The girls' bodies are primped, primed, and polished for *his* consumption and satisfaction.

Many people in modern cultures laud beauty and spa treatments because they provide relaxation and make customers more pleased with and confident about their bodies. But in contemporary economies of trafficking, beauty and spa services assist traffickers who intend to market and to cover up abuse, exploitation, and pain that may literally mark victims' bodies in physical and visible ways.[8] In the context of sexual trafficking, cosmetic treatments contribute to injury. They condition females to accept their own objectification and to undergo beautification for the gratification of consumers and perpetrators. Consequently, victims often internalize the perception that the abuse they suffer is acceptable. To read the text *without* identifying and critiquing mechanisms of sexual trafficking, or *without* connecting these to sexual trafficking of the past and present, readers and interpreters, albeit inadvertently, fail to acknowledge and resist ideological, cultural, and embodied sexual exploitation of girls and women. This exploitation, as explained, affects, and traumatizes especially and disproportionately females who are minoritized, including Africana females.

Applying the euphemism "beauty contest" to describe the exploitation of the virgin girls erases elements of trafficking, such as capture, captivity, and forced displacement, and prevents the analysis of such experiences as exploitative. Carol Bechtel notes that the descriptor is highly misleading, as contestants in beauty contests typically exercise volition (2002: 31). Bechtel also calls attention to the fact that, unlike contemporary beauty contest participants, the girls who are not chosen by Ahasuerus to be his new queen would have been unable to return home. The remaining girls become the king's concubines and remain sequestered in the king's harem indefinitely. Therefore, once raped and exploited in the narrative, African and other ethnic girls, including Indian and Persian girls, are narratively silenced and erased, similar to the way Vashti is erased. Sexual violence and exploitation, therefore, begin and end with narrative and vocal silencing and suppression. The girls of diverse ethnicities are victims of patriarchy and colonization, becoming the property of the empire, and (with the exception of Esther alone) all disappear into the narrative world, never to be mentioned again. Tsaurayi Mapfeka notes that the decision to replace Queen Vashti with young virgin women through a comprehensive and empire-wide search shows the empire's desire to assert absolute imperial power, authority, and control over its female population (2018: 86). More than this, however, the king's approval of the plan to expand his harem is nothing less than a royal sanction and legitimation of sexual trafficking.

Beauty, beautification, and pageants have become mechanisms of sex traffickers to facilitate crime. Traffickers capitalize on various cultures' obsessions with beauty and pageantry and use these themes/

processes to further mask and legalize exploitation and abuse. The injury and violence endured by the girls in the story world is obscured, in part, because law sanctions it. Many biblical interpreters, meanwhile, sanitize the exploitation of the girls as a harmless and "fun" beauty pageant, as I outlined above. In addition, the servants' tactics to force the girls into the king's palace and harem are often overlooked or downplayed. Instead, their role in sexual exploitation is framed as "facilitating" a better life for the girls, or as a mode of economic liberation, a way for them to escape poverty, and to rise through the social hierarchy by becoming queen. But it is imperative to resist framing the trafficking and abuse of the virgin girls in the book of Esther as fun, comical, advantageous, or as pageantry, as opposed to terrifying, legalized, systematic mass sexual abuse.

Edict-making is a recurring theme in the book of Esther. Not only do royal decrees include the language of violence, but they also play an unusual role in the story, because they are employed to carry out and to justify violence. The book is bracketed by edicts that sanction extensive and dreadful violence: in the beginning, the legal enforcement of female subservience, and, near the end of the book, an edict promulgating the institution of Purim, which is preceded by massacre. The only person who has full protection under law is the king (Stern 2015: 250).[9] The foiled plot by two angry eunuchs to assassinate him sees them impaled on stakes (2:21–23). Law ensures the king's inviolability, a privilege not afforded to any other character in the book, especially not the abducted African girls.

Both the law at the close of Esther 1 and the sexual trafficking of the virgin girls in the subsequent chapter are imposed upon the female collective, articulating the enormity of the consequences of one woman's disobedience and resistance to hegemonic masculinity and sexually abusive patriarchy. Both laws evoke terror and suffering among girls and women. To ensure male dominance and to secure patriarchal stability, the king and his officials use shame, fear, and sexual exploitation to correct and sustain gendered social control. In this way, law-making becomes a strategy that drives the violent plot of the narrative, commencing with the first two chapters and culminating with mass murder in the closing chapters of the text.

Law serves the king's interests in other ways. It procures him sexual partners and ensures he is physically guarded: no one is able to approach him without being summoned. He even creates a law for drinking to be unimpeded by law and settles a marital dispute by turning his wife's disobedience into imperial law for all wives. Craig Stern points out that in this context, law is shaped for utility. It is an instrument for the king and his advisers to mold the realm after royal will. The law is not concerned about justice or the common good; only the king's will and social objectives determine law (Stern 2015: 267). Persian law is thus a tool of power and domination that enacts unjust violence against vulnerable bodies (Stern 2015: 274).

The first two chapters of the book of Esther thus elucidate how imperial colonizers abuse their power to set up and enshrine systems of sexual trafficking, alongside other forms of systemic violence. The exploitations by the king and his imperial networks, along with the vulnerability and suffering of the virgin girls, are central for understanding sexual trafficking as a state-sanctioned and accepted form of sexual abuse. Notably, neither the abusive actions of those wielding power, nor the traumatic experience of the female victims is met with outrage or resistance by any of the characters in the story world. What exacerbates the physical violence that is condoned and promoted through edict-writing, is that Persian edicts are irrevocable (1:19). The fixity of Persian laws produces terror and fright for those whom the laws impact. For example, when females' subservience and inferiority is formalized, it extracts all agency and power from girls and women. Reflecting on Vashti's fate, it even renders resistance to their own objectification and humiliation illegal. Disempowerment and irrevocability stifle any resistance efforts or opportunities for social transformation and equity.

In the next section, I will outline tools of the king and other traffickers to lure abusees (through seduction and romance, sale by family/debt enslavement, and recruitment by former sex slaves) and to create obstacles to resistance (by means of isolation, power and control, naming/namelessness, invisibility, and language barriers).

Tools of sex traffickers: luring victims and barriers to resistance

Many factors contribute to children's vulnerability to trafficking.[10] Up to today, in many parts of the world, girls are coerced into sex work and trafficking on account of poverty and to secure protection from other forms of violence (Bryant-Davis et al. 2009: 81). Minoritized girls and women are at particular risk to these systemic factors, rendering them most vulnerable to sexual trafficking. Internationally, vast numbers of persons trafficked are of African, Asian, and Latin-American ancestry (Bryant-Davis et al. 2009: 71). The 2018 Trafficking in Persons Report confirms that the root causes of the crime of trafficking are "deeper that any one of its facets and relate to larger systemic conditions such as poverty, forced migration, racism, discrimination, among many others" (Trafficking in Persons Report 2018).

In addition, children and youth have even higher rates of sexual victimization than women or men. As criminologist and licensed mental health counselor Joan Reid points out,

> the young age of victims and their commensurate lack of psychosocial maturity cast doubt on their ability to detect exploitative motives or withstand manipulation of sex traffickers or recruiters. Due to inexperience and naiveté, minors are especially susceptible to sexual coercion and entrapment in juvenile sexual trafficking.
>
> (Reid 2016: 492)

Because of limited options and prospects, homeless and orphaned children are especially at risk. Traffickers prey on vulnerable victims, such as those who experience isolation and abandonment. Therefore, children in foster care or orphanages, who are runaways, or caught up in the juvenile justice systems, become prime targets for sexual trafficking. Perpetrators exploit vulnerabilities, lure, and groom children, to further isolate them from their families and communities. In Esther Chapter 2, the narrator explains, "Mordecai had brought up Hadassah, that is Esther, his cousin, for she had neither father nor mother; the girl was fair and beautiful, and when her father and her mother died, Mordecai adopted her as his own daughter" (2:7). Mordecai *'aman,* that is, supports, Hadassah, an exiled female Jewish orphan, as a foster parent. This detail might also hint at Esther's susceptibility to trafficking.

Living as foreigners in a diasporic community, Mordecai and Esther are descendants of captives carried away from their home in Jerusalem by King Nebuchadnezzar of Babylon (2:6). This detail provides further insight into their cultural and familial vulnerability to violence: experiences of displacement, alongside weakened family structures, coupled with Hadassah's age, gender, and orphan status all make her more prone to exploitation. Although she is not completely alone and defenseless, Hadassah, like Mordecai, is, as a member of a minority religious-ethnic-cultural group, prone to oppression or marginalization by the dominant colonizing Persians. Immersed in a patriarchal social setting, Hadassah is dependent on Mordecai's guardianship and protection, but even he may not be able to protect her from absorption into this horrendous system of sexual trafficking, on account of his own disenfranchisement and liminality. He may lack the cultural and/or financial capital to resist Persian imperial violence and oppression.

Moreover, traffickers sometimes threaten to kill or harm victims if their families are perceived as a threat.

Like many Africana girls and women vulnerable to exploitation, Hadassah is at a considerable disadvantage, because of her liminal status outside of conventional kinship structures. Helpless, she depends on personal protection, as well as legal protection. Her life is in jeopardy and her means of making a living is constrained. Caught in a web of patriarchal-sexist ideologies that promote rape culture and state-sanctioned exploitation, she is acutely vulnerable. Surviving in the context of legalized sexual oppression of ethnic minorities, Hadassah is economically dependent on her abuser. These conditions may have bearing, too, on her guardian's participation in her oppression. Comparable conditions exist for many African diasporic girls and women. Therefore, reading the story of Hadassah and the unnamed displaced virgin girls in light of contemporary manifestations of sexual trafficking, illuminates individual and collective Africana memories and identities also grounded in brutal socio-historical realities in which their bodies were and are exploited and abused.

In contemporary settings, children are drawn or lured into sexual trafficking systems because of their youth and other factors that render them vulnerable. Some have previous experiences of abandonment, or of physical, sexual, and other forms of abuse. Also, in situations of deprivation, families may sell children into trafficking structures. In both situations, traffickers take advantage of these conditions and often present themselves as empathetic and willing to help (Reid 2016: 492). Some victims are abducted and forced into trafficking. Other times, traffickers use recruiters to search for needy youth who are easily exploitable. Recruitment can be forced, or voluntary. In many instances, recruitment is facilitated by people unknown to the victim, including persons who are/have been subjected to sexual trafficking themselves. Sometimes, trafficked persons respond to economic pressures. At every stage, characterizing trafficking is not straightforward. As with notions of agency, notions of consent and recruitment are complex and complicated by power dynamics and structures. Circumstances and opportunities are context-specific, which necessitates nuance.

According to the Polaris Project, traffickers can be family members or strangers, who, having identified vulnerable targets, often make false promises to address or fulfill their targets' needs. This serves to lure targets. Traffickers promise access to love, safety, attention, education, travel, good jobs, citizenship in another country, money-making schemes, marriage proposals, among other tempting opportunities, to win victims' trust. Tactics can include seduction and romance, false job advertisements, and also bullying, threats, abduction, and sale by family (Reid 2016: 492).[11] The most common form of recruitment is through debt bondage, wherein victims are forced to pledge labor or other services, to repay a form of debt, such as living expenses, the cost of procuring travel documents, or transportation (including smuggle) to a foreign country (Hodge 2008: 143–152). Most relevant to the book of Esther are seduction and romance, sale by family, debt slavery, and recruitment by former sexual slaves.

The method of seduction and romance includes a highly deceptive form of grooming and abuse. Traffickers, also known as "lover boys," form romantic relationships with targets, which lead to emotionally, psychologically, physically, and sexually abusive relationships. Romancing includes showing off wealth, buying gifts, and spending money on young adolescent girls to make them feel desired and loved (Reid 2016: 497–498). The lover boy also uses violence to intimidate his victims into compliance. In the book of Esther, after the king abducts the girls, grooming takes the form of the long, lavish beautification process leading up to rape.

Reid also notes that lover boys use flattery and hyperbole, painting a picture of a wonderful life together, to isolate victims from and persuade them to leave their families and associates. Undoubtedly, the detailed narration of the stately decor and the alluring descriptions of the king's palace in Chapter 1 reflect a similar kind of showing off. The material resources of the king and the grandeur of his kingdom signify access to desirable resources, wealth, and power. Once Esther becomes queen, she indeed gains access to some of these vestiges. The other girls, however, do not, because as concubines, they fall lower down on the social hierarchical spectrum. Like Vashti, they, too, disappear from the narrative.

Conditions such as destitute poverty, displacement, forced exile, and diasporic living can lead to desperation. Sometimes, families sell their children out of desperate economic necessity, or in the hope of procuring for them a better life. Nehemiah 5 details some economic hardships endured in the Persian Empire. Debt slavery is depicted as a widespread problem. People report selling their children and hiring out their labor to pay off debt because they have no other means.[12] Although both daughters and sons are sold as slaves, daughters are sold before sons (Nehemiah 5:5; Westbrook 1995: 1645). Sadly, such desperation prevails in modern times. Families today, too, sell their children into slavery and sex work to alleviate or escape cycles of poverty. Furthermore, attitudes to sexual trafficking are not always negative. Some families engage in sexual trafficking because it is a lucrative business. Multiple generations participate and are raised in a culture that deems sexual trafficking acceptable, or at least tolerable or defensible. Health professionals Okonofua et al. performed a study wherein 47% of participants believed that there are positive benefits to sexual trafficking, including that it brings wealth to families, improves their standard of living, and provides visibility (2004: 1322). For all the negative tolls that sexual trafficking undoubtedly exacts on individuals' bodies and psyches, ambiguities of power and a lack of viable or preferable alternatives can also lead persons to perceive sexual trafficking and sex work as having positive benefits, especially for families and local economies.

Some contemporary victims of trafficking internalize the violence and exploitation they have experienced and become allies with their abusers. Helping perpetrators recruit other victims can result from trusting traffickers over and against others. Of significance here is the role of the eunuchs in the narrative world and trafficking system of Esther. This is where the virgin girls and the eunuchs converge in the book of Esther; both are victims of the king's sexual exploitation and abuse. Bailey illustrates that the eunuchs and servants who "attend" the king are sexually exploited by him in the same manner as the virgin girls. The verb *šrt* (1:10; 2:2; 6:3) translated as "to attend" signifies sexual activity (2009: 237).[13] Bailey's exposure of this abuse might shed light on why the servants make the suggestion to seek young virgins for the king: *they too are victims of the king's sexual exploitation.* They are the king's sex slaves who become partners with the king, aiding him in gaining access to other vulnerable bodies.

Vern Bullough, historian and sexologist, notes that eunuchs are sexually ambiguous and through castration, bear permanent physical wounds (literally, *stigma)* that relegate them to socially constructed identities of shame and exclusion (2002: 1). There are many reasons why men might be castrated: to exert control, domination, or punishment, for political, religious, sexual, or medical/health reasons. One prominent reason is control. Cyrus the Great of Persia writes of his rationale for eunuchs:

> For instance, vicious horses, when gelded, stop biting and prancing about, to be sure, but are none the less fit for service in war; and bulls, when castrated, lose somewhat of their high spirit and unruliness but are not deprived of their strength or capacity to work. And in the same way dogs, when castrated, stop running away from their masters, but are no less useful for watching or hunting. And men, too, in the same way, become gentler when

deprived of this desire, but not less careful of that which is en-
trusted to them.

(Xenophon Cyropaedia 1914: 289)

In cultures where masculine males are valued for sexual prowess and
virility, emasculation symbolizes shame, impotence, and social marginalization. Imperialists not infrequently penetrate, brand, maim, or
otherwise mark the bodies of those they oppress – to reduce the threat
they pose and to make them compliant. Sexual colonizing of bodies
also renders these bodies pliable for prolonged exploitation (Heath
2001: 89–90). This applies to the eunuchs *and* to the raped girls.

The eunuchs give us a hint as to their own experiences of violent sexual exploitation when they suggest that the king seeks out and gathers
the girls (2:2–3) and when Hegai advises them how to perform in the
king's bedroom (2:15). Because of their royal office and proximity to
the king, eunuchs are weaponized to assist in the trafficking enterprise:
they simultaneously guard and instruct the girls (2:13–15). Bailey cites
sociologist Orlando Patterson, who argues that not all slavery involves
labor exploitation. Rather, slavery is primarily a "relation of ritualized
humiliation and dishonor" (Patterson 1982: 77–101) and exploitation
takes multiple forms. The eunuchs were made into sex slaves and go
on to groom the girls for sex work, even if this results in humiliation
and dishonor for both collectives. Both become symbols of abject degradation (Willis 1998: 27) and the enslavement of both is due as much
to internalized degradation as the sex work itself.

The king has physical and sexual access to the eunuchs, who, on the
one hand, are degraded and emasculated. But the eunuchs also have
some power and privilege, such as uninhibited access to the girls and
women belonging to the king. As persons of liminal sex, neither male
nor female, eunuchs live in a world inhabited by the king's women
without posing any threat to him (Llewellyn-Jones 2002: 19). Further,
eunuchs act as a set of eyes and ears that operate outside of the confines
of the domestic heart of the palace, relaying official messages between
the inner and outer courts, along with unofficial gossip, scandals, and
secrets (Llewellyn-Jones 2002: 29). Lloyd Llewellyn-Jones also claims
Hegai's devotions and unfailing loyalty make him the perfect product
of harem society (2002: 19–20): a product of such, Hegai knows well,
from experience, the type and scope of abuse that the king is capable
of (2002: 35).

Llewellyn-Jones defines the harem as a physical space, or identifia-
ble area of the palace, used by women, eunuchs, and certain privileged
men. It is a space that describes something that is "out of bounds" or

forbidden. He writes, "by implication, it means a space into which the general access is forbidden (or limited) and in which the presence of certain individuals or certain types of behaviors are forbidden" (2002: 25). Again, this underscores the role of eunuchs as guards to the king's girls and women, because the king does not want any male to gain sexual access to them. The denotation of "harem" then, is a place of hiding and concealment – and hiding and concealment are crucial for facilitating sexual trafficking.

Harem infrastructures in the ancient context have parallels with hotspots in contemporary contexts. Not only are the virgin girls sequestered into a sexual trafficking ring in Susa, but Hegai also advises Hadassah as to what she should do to win favor with the king. In other words, the eunuch tells her how to use the exploitation of her body to secure her position as queen. All the men who encounter Hadassah in this narrative exploit her.[14] But the other girls and the eunuchs are also stripped of agency and honor when sexually abused by the king. Attention to both collectives is necessary, because, as Llewellyn-Jones points out, women and servants, especially eunuchs, too often fade into the background of androcentric Persian royal texts (2002: 22). He suggests that the royal harem may be the battleground of the empire, where great men rise and fall and are manipulated by women and eunuchs (2002: 23). But what seems likelier is that girls, women, and eunuchs are viciously manipulated, exploited, and abused *by* the empire. *Their bodies* are the battlegrounds upon which imperial wars manifest.

Yet another mechanism of sexual trafficking and a barrier to resistance is victim isolation. The text implies the virgin girls' isolation from their families. With the exception of Hadassah, all the girls remain secluded in the king's harem. Because Hadassah pleases Hegai and wins his favor, he (expeditiously!) provides her with not only cosmetics, rations, and seven chosen maids but also with special kindness (2:9). And so, when the girls are gathered, Mordecai, sitting at the king's gate (2:19), can walk around to the front of the court of the harem every day to learn how Hadassah fares (2:11). Undoubtedly, he can do so by building a relationship with the eunuchs who guard the threshold. In this way, Mordecai learns about how two of them, Bigthan and Teresh, plot to assassinate the king, and he relays this to Hadassah who, in turn, conveys it to the king in Mordecai's name (2:21–22). These details show that Mordecai has access to Hadassah, unlike the family members of the other victims.

Moreover, criminologists note that hot spot establishments often have security measures to prevent victims from escaping and to protect victims from outside attacks by other criminals.[15] In the book of Esther, the narrator reveals that two eunuchs function in the role of guards to the virgin girls: Hegai is "in charge of the women" (2:3) and Shaashgaz is "in charge of the concubines" (2:14). *Shamar,* translated as "guard" in the NRSV, means "to guard, protect, or attend to" (BDB, entry 8104). When the virgin girls are first brought to the king's palace, they are put under Hegai's custody due to their virginal status. Then, once the king debases and devalues the girls through non-consensual sex, the girls are transported to a second harem where the king's concubines are housed under the custody of Shaashgaz.

Victims are sometimes kept in hot spots for extended periods of time or are rotated to other locations to ensure their safety from outsiders and/or to prevent perpetrators from being caught by law enforcement. This is evidenced in the text when the girls are rotated to different locales within the king's palace and kept there indefinitely. Unfortunately, in the ancient context, there is a conflation of imperial and legal authorities. The king and his officials both construct and enforce the laws. Thus, the girls are trapped and no outside entity can protect them from the imperially commissioned and sanctioned sexual trafficking.

Hegai and Shaashgaz are primarily responsible for ensuring that the virgin girls, wives, and concubines are safe in the harem. However, a later scene reveals that the king has the capacity to protect his property from outside threats, too. When the king believes that Haman is assaulting Esther, because he throws himself in supplication on the couch where Esther is reclining, the king commands for Haman to be hanged on the gallows he had prepared for Mordecai (7:7–9). The king does not have Haman hanged because Esther exposed his plot to kill her people. Rather, the king commands Haman's execution because he perceives Haman as an outside threat to "his" woman: Queen Esther, whom the king had selected for his own and exclusive sexual pleasure.

Also typical of contemporary manifestations of sexual trafficking, while at hot spots, traffickers instill fear in their victims, confiscate their personal goods and identifications, and therewith isolate them further from their families and make escape harder. The narrator neglects to report any interior feelings of the girls as they experience movement from their homes to the king's palace and motion within the palace. However, one can imagine the fear a child endures on being removed from her home, her parents, or guardians, and from everything she had experienced as familiar, to a place where everything is unknown and uncertain.

Children are frequently attached to items such as blankets or toys, which give them a sense of comfort, familiarity, security, and familial belonging. The narrator does not detail whether the girls bring any personal belongings to the king's palace. The only reference to a possession is what the girls ask for and are given to take with them from the harem to the king's bedroom (2:13). These girls are children. Rather than being given child-appropriate toys, they are groomed and given sex toys. To remove children from their homes and not allow them access to items that sustain their sense of identity may constitute a double loss and multiple traumas. Access to and withdrawal from these items can have profound emotional effects on victims, which is why perpetrators sometimes use them to manipulate and their control victims (Chinn 2013: 117).

Traffickers isolate victims from their homes and families in part to create leverage and dependency. By denying or thwarting access, perpetrators disrupt communication, minimize resistance on both sides (victims and victims' families), and maximize their control over the situation. Precisely because Esther is *not* fully isolated from her relative and guardian (2:7), she and Mordecai are able to collaborate and save the Jews when the threat of genocide looms. However, Mordecai apparently does nothing to help Hadassah escape the sexual exploitation she endures in the palace – possibly because he can draw benefit from it. The other nameless girls who are also held prisoner are entirely isolated, with no hope of return to their families or communities. Like many other victims of sexual trafficking, they are cut off from their loved ones and the outside world, interminably.

Separation and isolation from families and wider communities are a couple of ways that traffickers assert power and control over abusees. Power and control wheels elucidate the various tactics that abusers utilize to manipulate relationships through control and power and detail types of abuse that victims of sexual trafficking endure in contemporary contexts.[16] Inside of the wheel is a set of behaviors often considered "red flags," signaling forms of control, manipulation, and violence. In the story world, this includes sexual, economic, and emotional abuse, isolation, and using privilege to gain access to and to abuse the virgin girls. The outer ring represents types of victimization and trafficking. These patterns can also be identified in the ancient context. The king and his collaborators define gender roles and legally enforce female subservience. After victims are abducted, traffickers use their power to keep their victims under strict control and surveillance. The king does this by appointing his eunuchs as guards over the females in his palace. Bailey writes, "It is in this act of requiring teenage girls, brought in from provinces all throughout his kingdom, to have sex with him, that the king uses sex and sexuality as a major tool of social control and manipulation" (Bailey 2009: 237). Modern traffickers further leverage victims' vulnerabilities through strategies such as debilitation, dread, and by creating dependency, which make victims controllable and limit their mental and physical capacity to resist. In the text, the king and his officials create dependency upon him and his empire. In this way, sexual violence, exploitation, and trafficking are normalized, which is the foundation of rape culture.

Names, namelessness, what the abused are called and choose to call themselves, and silencing are other features of sexual trafficking that should not be ignored, because they are weaponized against abusees to sustain trafficking systems and cultures. In many cases, victims of sexual trafficking are not addressed by their legal names. They may be identified by derogatory slang terms, such as bitch, whore, or trick, which, intentionally and strategically rob them of personhood and contribute to their dehumanization. It prevents victims from developing a sense of dignity and self-identity, which can result in self-detachment. Children, especially when they encounter stressful events such as severe or prolonged sexual abuse and exploitation, dissociate psychologically for self-protection and to escape when they cannot protect themselves (Cruz 2016).

There are very many names in the book of Esther, but Hadassah is the only captured girl who is named. Both her Jewish *and* Persian names are disclosed: Hadassah is her Jewish name, and Esther is her Persian name (2:7). The only other two named females are Vashti (Chapter 1) and Zeresh, Haman's wife (5:14, 6:13). Females are comparatively rarely mentioned by name in the Bible. Only two eponymous books are named for women: Esther and Ruth. In the book of Esther, the narrator reveals that the king summons a girl by name if he delights in her but none of their names are ever recorded (2:14). The unnamed virgin girls are narratively depicted in ways similar to other African female characters in the Bible. For example, Potiphar's wife (Genesis 39), Moses's Cushite wife (Numbers 12), the Queen of Sheba (1 Kings 10), and many of Solomon's wives, including a daughter of Pharaoh (1 Kings 3:1), are all nameless African women. Moreover, there are likely to have been in Israel's history, alongside named African sexual slaves, such as Hagar, many more unnamed African slaves.

Namelessness and invisibility (e.g., facelessness), along with constant movement, prevent identification and tracking of victims. These methods enable traffickers to orchestrate systematic rape on a large scale under the radar and to avoid getting caught. The virgin girls are not the only females that are nameless in Chapter 2. The wives and concubines under the custody of Hegai and Shaashgaz are nameless as well. Although the narrator does not reveal how many wives and concubines the king has, readers can assume that their number is large, given his ability to gather girls from all over his vast kingdom. The distinction between wives and concubines further underscores a hierarchy, as well as levels of abuse perpetrated by imperial power. To give some sense of the magnitude, biblical historian Llewellyn-Jones proposes that the number of women constituting a royal harem could be in excess of 400 at any one time (2002: 31).

Wives, although limited by patriarchal and kyriarchal social orders, had more voice, agency, power, and resources than concubines and non-married women. This may be why Vashti and Esther, both of whom are named, speak (although Vashti's words are relayed through an intermediary), and act, while the other virgin girls do not. What is interesting, though, is that Esther is granted resources and is advanced by Hegai even *before* she becomes queen. Contemporary victims of sexual trafficking are frequently denied or granted food and other resources as punishment and reward respectively. If Esther becomes queen because she is best able to sexually satisfy the king (denoted in the text by the word "please") is she afforded these resources earlier because she sexually "pleases" Hegai as well (2:9)? If so, it appears that the king is not the only perpetrator. Perhaps, Hegai also sexually exploits Esther.

A deeper exploration of the meaning of Hadassah's names further elucidates her experiences and interactions with imperial powers. "Hadassah" is derived from Hebrew *hadas,* meaning "myrtle" or "pleasing of scent" (BDB, entry 1918). Myrtle trees have white flowers that are used to create perfume and are a symbol of love and marriage. Myrtle trees are also used to make wreaths in wedding ceremonies.[17] The name Hadassah, therefore, prefigures her fate as the replacement queen. Her Jewish name reflects her status as honored and favored in this diasporic setting, as evidenced already by her gaining the favor of Hegai. This is confirmed by her winning over the king, and by her subsequent ascension as queen.[18]

"Esther," on the other hand, is Hadassah's Persian name. It means "star" and is associated with Ishtar, the goddess of war and sexual love. It, too, foreshadows Esther's experiences: this time, of violence through sexual exploitation, as the king weaponizes sex against her and the other virgin girls. Ishtar is characterized as young, beautiful, courageous, and impulsive, corresponding with descriptions of Esther in the text. Moreover, one of Isthar's legacies is that she is a protector of sex workers. She is described as having priestess-sex workers, who in later times were virgins not permitted to marry ("Ishtar,"

Encyclopedia Britannica, 2018). Esther may serve in this capacity as protector of the other females under the king's authority since she is coerced into becoming the protector of the Jews and fulfills the task successfully.

The name Esther also corresponds to the Hebrew *hester,* which means "hiddenness" (BDB, entry 5641). In the text, Esther conceals her ethnic identity. Conversations about hiddenness in the book of Esther usually pertain to the hiddenness of God in the text. Yet, it is congruous also with the hiddenness of the virgin girls, trafficked into and concealed in the king's palace. Rachel Adelman maintains the wordplay between *hester* and Esther constructs Esther and her world as embodying the terror represented by God's hidden face foreshadowed in Deuteronomy (31:17–18): in Esther's time, God hides, bringing "terrible troubles" (2014: 89). Not only is God's face hidden, but the virgin girls' names and faces remain hidden, too. After the second chapter, they completely disappear from the story.

Jo Carruthers, professor of literature and Bible, suggests that Esther is the name of the queen and Hadassah is the name of the maiden girl (2009: 66). By making this distinction, Carruthers illuminates her dual identities that operate in different social settings. This observation may provide evidence of a psychological split of self, resulting from trauma. Hadassah/Esther is constantly negotiating multiple identities. This is compounded by Mordecai instructing Esther to hide her Jewish ethnic identity to pass as Persian. Not only does this contribute to Hadassah/Esther's split identity, but it fosters ethnic suppression and invisibility as well, both of which are used as tools of traffickers in contemporary settings.

Although contemporary victims of sexual trafficking are often isolated their families, many cultivate relationships with other victims, based on shared experiences of isolation and exploitation. Attention to other terms that describe victims of sexual trafficking sheds light on how victims of trafficking are defined and understood by perpetrators and other persons in power, and how victims understand themselves and their relationship to other victims. There are various terms used to describe victims under the same pimp. These terms reflect both societal and cultural views about victims, as well as victims' views and understandings of themselves and co-victims. One term that picks up on the inferiority and dehumanization of females is "stable" which signifies a group of women under the control of a single pimp. This term symbolizes the ways that girls and women are marked and treated as chattel or cattle (that is, as commodities and non-human animals) in contemporary contexts. Stables, after all, are basic structures wherein livestock or horses are housed, kept, and trained. Trafficked *humans* are brought into hot spots, kept, and trained how to be sexually exploited by perpetrators. The book of Esther reflects this concept. The virgin girls are brought into and kept in the king's palace. Moreover, there is an explicit reference to Hegai advising or training Esther on what will happen in the king's bedroom (2:15a).

In contemporary contexts, many victims create bonds based on shared experiences of oppression. Sometimes, however, cultural and language barriers obstruct the development of bonding, which has the potential to undermine attempts at collaboration and resistance. In the first chapter of Esther, the narrator reveals that the people across the provinces speak diverse languages, noting that the king sends letters "to all the royal provinces in its own script and to every people in its own language" (1:22). The narrator confirms repeatedly that the people throughout the king's provinces do not speak a common language (3:12; 8:9). Language barriers such as those identified in the book of Esther might prevent victims of exploitation from supporting each other, reaching out for help, or resisting the exploitative behaviors of the king and other parties.

Although some girls in the story world may have been able to relate to and communicate with others, diverse languages can contribute to victim isolation and inhibit attempts of victims' collective action. This certainly draws parallels with separation and isolation practices among contemporary colonizers, who intentionally put people of different language backgrounds together to limit communication and therewith prevent organized resistance. While cultural and language barriers do not necessarily prevent victims from perceiving or considering each other as family/kin or bonded, it limits the ways and extent that victims can interact meaningfully. Adelman notes three aspects of an authoritarian regime that I see represented in the narrative: the role of dressing up as objects of desire in another's eyes (e.g., dressing up the virgins and, in the case of Vashti, seeking to show off her *undressed* body); the consequent exile of self and identity; and lastly, the subversion of language for the oppressed community (2014: 87).

Adelman also emphasizes another issue concerning language by pointing out that possibly, Vashti's mother tongue is forbidden in her own home, rendering her tongue-tied (2014: 86). This demonstrates another layer of complexity regarding experiences of sexual trafficking and tools of traffickers: the erasure of ethnic and cultural identity markers. Victims are often able to preserve aspects of their identities through languages because their beliefs, values, and worldviews are embedded within language. If, once Esther becomes queen, she is made to abandon her mother tongue and to appropriate the imperial language, this will contribute to her identity crisis. Loss of language is not just a loss of culture and of identity but is a loss of subjectivity as it impedes the transmission of experiences, traditions, and knowledge (Borossa 1998: 391–402). When a language is erased, so are the ethnic and cultural histories and heritages that accompany it. Erasure and suppression of language is a form of ethnic cleansing widely practiced in colonial contexts that further thwarts individual and collective resistance to violence and oppression.

Even though females in the text are often silenced, narratively erased, many unnamed, and identified in relation to men – as wives, concubines, and virgins (i.e., potential wives and concubines) – the female collective plays an important narrative role. These characters are indeed central to the plot development. Moreover, when interpreters choose to prioritize the female characters and to read the narrative through the lenses of intersectionality and collective trauma, then sexual trafficking comes to the fore of the interpretative process. Instead of reading the abuse as a harmless beauty contest, interpreters may be able to perceive these girls as subjected to a much more horrendous encounter of sexual exploitation.

After her "one night with the king" and subsequent appointment as queen of Persia, Mordecai says to Esther, perhaps you've have come to royal dignity for "such a time as this" (4:14b). We cannot afford to over spiritualize these phrases or continue to ignore and minimize what happens during Hadassah's and the other virgin girls' one night with the king. Why are readers and hearers taught to celebrate one night with the king? In doing so, do we inadvertently suggest that a female's purpose and/or destiny is to prepare herself for one night of sex in order to possibly advance in life? If we continue to trivialize the phrases "one night with the king" or "for such a time as this," we risk failing to see the other part of "this": Esther not only has to rise to advocate on behalf of and save her people, the Jews, during this "time" but she also must endure sexualize abuse for four lengthy years, which is such a long time, to even have a chance at becoming a queen, a position that affords her the power and privilege to aid the Jews in the first place.

The namelessness and invisibility of the African and other virgin girls stand out even more when juxtaposed with the admiration and dignity conferred on Esther (2:15b). Hadassah is visible, and her visibility is heightened when the king places the crown upon her head (2:17) and presents her as the replacement of Vashti. She later uses her power and visibility to challenge and change conditions that threatened the lives and livelihood of the Jews. Although "invisabilized" and silenced, the other virgin girls also spend one night with the king. Perhaps readers and interpreters have been chosen "for such a time as this," to #SayHerName, say their names, share their stories, and to aid these nameless, faceless girls just as Esther did for the Jews.

Deliberate attention focused on the other girls in the text makes visible what has been historically rendered invisible and silent: that is, the voices and experiences of countless African(a) girls and women caught in sexual trafficking. Attention to "invisibalized" African girls in the story world also allows interpreters to analyze the mechanisms that produce such invisibility and silence. Exegesis of this book that leads to interpreting the actions of the king and the Persian Empire as exploitative and trauma-inducing might provide religious scholars and leaders insights, tools, and the courage to call out and hold accountable social, religious, and legal institutions that facilitate and perpetuate trafficking specifically, and rape culture, more broadly. What should we be prepared to do in this time? My intersectional polyvocal interpretation of Esther may very well poise readers to discern if this is a "for such a time as this" moment for us, to call out the trafficking, sexual exploitation, and narrative and historical erasure of Africana and other females impacted by sexualized violence. Just as we evaluate the conditions that necessitates Hadassah stepping up to lead, we must discern the conditions that compel our stepping up as leaders in cultures marked by colonialism, patriarchy, and rape. That's what the #SayHerName movement affords us the space to do as we engage the biblical texts.

Intersectionality and polyvocality spotlight the trauma of African girls who are embedded in this story of Israel's past. The gender, social, and cultural restrictions experienced by African characters who live in a world intertwined with other minoritized and exploited girls, as well as with their oppressors, come together in the book of Esther. Bringing ancient text into dialogue with realities of the present illuminates both settings.

In Chapter 2, I focus on another major strand of sexual trafficking, facilitated during the Maafa, paying attention to the role of intersectionality in Africana girls' and women's abuse and how the above-outlined issues shaped the lives of those captured and trafficked. I illustrate that trafficking demands boundary transgression of multiple types: including bodily, spatial, and geographical. In addition, I posit that the sexual abuse facilitated during the Maafa created a class of sex slaves and is a site of collective memory for Africana diasporized females. Moreover, collective memory affords members of the collective opportunities to address past and present challenges and needs so that they can process the many acts of trauma that they continue to endure and transform the imposed stigma and shame into productive energy that will enable them to continue to survive and thrive as a collective.

Notes

1 Feminist philosopher, social theorist, and political activist Simone de Beauvoir posits that "woman" represents the quintessential expression of "other." Because women represent the opposite of men, men differentiate and discriminate against women. Famously, de Beauvoir asserted, "one is not born, but rather becomes, a woman." Hence, gender is a socially constructed and assigned aspect of identity. Moreover, males' self-definition and differentiation requires a contrast to another that devalues what is relative to them. De Beauvoir further maintains that female embodiment has advantages and disadvantages. The female body is an ambiguous site, as it embodies both oppression and freedom simultaneously. Woman is both the object of society's gaze, and a free subject. Consequently, women use their bodies as vehicles for freedom *and* feel also oppressed by them. These observations become significant when considering the role that gender plays in the formulation of "otherness" in the book of Esther and in Ancient Near Eastern culture. See, Simone de Beauvoir, *The Second Sex* (New York: Vintage Books, 1974).
2 Defining kyriarchy, Elisabeth Schüssler Fiorenza describes and differentiates power in terms of the status of freeborn lord *(kyrios)* or lady *(kyria)* and in terms of class, colonial, and race status. She notes how colonization, race, and class are intersectional modes of domination and oppression in kyriarchal power, unlike in analyses of patriarchal power. See, *Congress of Wo/men: Religion, Gender and Kyriarchal Power* (Cambridge: Feminist Studies in Religion Books, 2016).
3 The society depicted in the biblical text portrays kyriarchy: a governance whereby kings and patriarchs exclude both freeborn and enslaved wo/men from full citizenship and decision-making. This form of governance enables the king and members of his imperial court to socially construct what it means to embody masculinity and femininity; to define and demarcate females and gender-bending males (eunuchs) as "the Other;" to legalize hegemonic male superiority and female inferiority; to banish Queen Vashti for her resistance to male-defined and -imposed femininity; and then to collect and sexually exploit girls and women and to dispose of or seclude them in the king's harem indefinitely.
4 See map of the Persian Empire on *Bible Odyssey:* https://www.bibleodyssey.org/tools/map-gallery/p/persian-empire; Note: Ethiopia and India are not represented on the map, although they are named in the text. The Achaemenid Persians built a vast empire. However, there are no maps that list Ethiopia as one of the provinces. Roland Kent maintains that Ethiopia was not likely part of a satrapy but exchanged goods with Persian officials, which has been confirmed by inscriptions at Darius's palace (See R. G. Kent, *Old Persian Grammar, Texts, Lexicon,* 2nd Rv. Ed., New Haven,

CT: American Oriental Society, 1953). However, A. Shapur Shahbazi notes that the Persians conquered parts of Ethiopia. Shahbazi cites Darius's state as the first world empire that extended "from Sogdiana by the Aral Sea, and the Punjab Valley of the Indus all the way to the Danube, Cyprus, Libya and Ethiopia..." See A. Shapur Shahbazi, "The Achaemenid Persian Empire (550–330 BCE)," in *The Oxford Handbook of Iranian History,* edited by Touraj Daryaee (Oxford; New York: Oxford University Press, 2012). By failing to include Ethiopia as one of the provinces of the Persian empire, this map is symbolic of yet another type of narrative erasure that Africana and other minoritized women experience daily.

5 Middle English "brothel" means "worthless man, prostitute" related to the Old English *brēothan,* "degenerate, deteriorate." Interestingly, the semantics reflect worthlessness of the male; however, when girls are trafficked, worthlessness and shame are shifted to female victims.

6 Duran, "Who Wants to Marry a Persian King?," 77–78.

7 Oil is associated with fatness, anointing, and fruitfulness, and perfume with sweetness. Oil and perfume are artifacts that symbolize honor and status; the use of them obscures the objectification of the girls and conceals how the beautification process contributes to their abuse. The allusion to fruitfulness might point to the prevalence of contemporary experiences of unwanted pregnancies and abortions among victims of sexual trafficking. Similarly, the reference to "purification" signals concurrent implications of sexually transmitted diseases and infections caused by sexual exploitation.

8 See, Karen Francis, "The Face of Resilience: Beauty Brands Come Together in Support of Human Trafficking Survivors," *The Root,* May 8, 2019, accessed July 24, 2019, https://theglowup.theroot.com/the-face-of-resilience-beauty-brands-come-together-in-1826088559; "A Black Owned Natural Beauty Brand Existing to End Human Trafficking," *Melanin and Sustainable Style,* December 29, 2017, accessed July 16, 2021 https://melaninass.com/blog/2017/12/28/ehno3u7gjafzgdlqt89099f4odpn7m?rq=Human%20 Trafficking

9 Craig Stern emphasizes that law establishes the reign and the king's provinces. See, "Megillath Esther and the Rule of Law: Disobedience and Obligation," in *Rutgers Journal of Law and Religion,* Vol. 17 (2015): 250 [n 14].

10 Among them are: age, poverty, weakened family structures, desire to migrate, political instability, socioeconomic status, childhood sexual abuse, family pressure for girls to sacrifice themselves for the survival of their families, and cultural norms regarding gender role ideologies,. All of these operate in various ways to obscure and justify acts of sexual assault. See, Thema Bryant-Davis et al., "Millennium Abolitionists," 69–78.

11 See, "Human Trafficking," Polaris Project, accessed on July 9, 2019, https://polarisproject.org/victims-traffickers.

12 See Deuteronomy 15:12–18; 2 Kings 4:1; Nehemiah 5:1–19 and Raymond Westbrook, "Slave and Master in Ancient Near Eastern Law," in *Chicago-Kent Law Review* Vol. 70, no. 4 (June 1995): 1631–1676, 1635. See also Gregory C. Chirichigno (ed.), *Debt-Slavery in Israel and the Ancient Near East* (Sheffield: Sheffield Academic Press, 1993). Joseph, whose story has some parallels with Esther's, is a kidnap victim sold into slavery (Genesis

37:12–36). Joseph, too, is at risk of sexual harassment and exploitation (Genesis 39).

13 According to Bailey, *šrt* is used in 1 Kings 1:4, to describe sexual activity with reference to David and Abishag (cf. the sexual tension where a word of this root appears in 2 Samuel 13:9). See Randall C. Bailey, "That's Why They Didn't Call the Book Hadassah!": The Interse(ct)/(x)ionality of Race/Ethnicity, Gender, and Sexuality in the Book of Esther," in *They Were All Together in One Place? Toward Minority Biblical Criticism*, edited by Randall Bailey, Tat-Siong Benny Liew, and Fernando Segovia (Atlanta: Society of Biblical Literature, 2009), 237.

14 Adelman claims Esther is taken forcibly three times: by Mordecai as a daughter, then to the king's palace by the officers (along with all the other virgins), and next by the king in marriage, reflecting a "unilateral male assertion of the possession of the woman," 87.

15 In trafficking discourse, and in the term "hotspot" also indicates routes or circuits where higher concentrations of sexual trafficking take place. In criminology and legal terms, "hotspots" denote places with higher concentrations of crime. Criminologists are shifting the focus from "hotspots" to "harmspots," to illuminate the impact of crimes not only on place and space but on human subjects. This shift in focus from the crime to the impact of the crime aids in our ability to understand the geospatial, economic, and social impacts of sexual trafficking on victims and on the communities from which they come and to which they are transplanted. See Cristobal Weinborn, Barak Ariel, Lawrence W. Sherman, and Emma O'Dwyer, "Hotspots vs. Harmspots: Shifting the Focus from Counts to Harm in the Criminology of Place," in *Applied Geography* Vol. 86 (2017): 226–244.

16 See, for example, the Trafficking Power and Control Wheel created by the Polaris Project: https://polarisproject.org/how-human-trafficking-happens/power-and-control-wheel/. This wheel is an adaptation of the Power and Control Wheel created by the staff at the Domestic Abuse Intervention Project (DAIP) located in Duluth, MN. The original wheel was created to illustrate the lived experiences of battered individuals, and to develop a curriculum for explaining domestic violence to batterers, the battered, practitioners within the criminal justice center, and members of the wider community. See: https://www.theduluthmodel.org/wheels/faqs-about-the-wheels/.

17 "What does the Name Hadassah Mean?" *Chabad*, accessed May 26, 2019, https://www.chabad.org/library/article_cdo/aid/1769366/jewish/What-Does-the-Name-Hadassah-Mean.htm; "Wedding Wreaths," Harper's Weekly, Vol. 46: 446.

18 In Zechariah, myrtles are also associated with righteousness (1:8). The sages in midrash suggest that Esther is good to Mordecai, who is portrayed as righteous throughout the narrative (Rabbah 6:5).

Works Cited

Adelman, Rachel. "'Passing Strange' – Reading Transgender across Genre: Rabbinic Midrash and Feminist Hermeneutics on Esther." *Journal of Feminist Studies in Religion* 30, no. 2 (2014): 81–97.

Bailey, Randall C. "That's Why They Didn't Call the Book Hadassah!": The Interse(ct)/(x)ionality of Race/Ethnicity, Gender, and Sexuality in the Book of Esther." In *They Were All Together in One Place? Toward Minority Biblical Criticism.* Randall Bailey, Tat-Siong Benny Liew, and Fernando Segovia, eds. Atlanta: Society of Biblical Literature, 2009: 227–250.

Bechtel, Carol. *Esther, Interpretation: A Bible Commentary for Teaching and Preaching.* Louisville: John Knox Press, 2002.

Beyer, Nancy. "The Sex Tourism Industry Spreads to Costa Rica and Honduras: Are These Countries Doing Enough to Protect Their Children from Sexual Exploitation." *Georgia Journal of International & Comparative Law* 29 (2001): 301–333.

Borossa, Julia. "Identity, Loss and the Mother Tongue." *Paragraph: A Journal of Modern Critical Theory* 21, no. 3 (November 1998): 391–402.

Brown, Francis, S. R. Driver, Charles A. Briggs, James Strong, and Wilhelm Gesenius. *The Brown-Driver-Briggs Hebrew and English Lexicon: With an Appendix Containing the Biblical Aramaic: Coded with the Numbering System from Strong's Exhaustive Concordance of the Bible.* Peabody, MA: Hendrickson Publishers, 1996.

Bryant-Davis, Thema, Shaquita Tillman, Alison Marks, and Kimberly Smith. "Millennium Abolitionists: Addressing the Sexual Trafficking of African Women." *Beliefs and Values* 1, no. 1 (2009): 69–78.

Bullough, Vern. "Eunuchs in History and Society." In *Eunuchs in Antiquity and Beyond.* Shaun Tougher, ed. London: The Classic Press of Wales, 2002: 1–17.

Carruthers, Jo. "Writing, Interpretation, and the Book of Esther: A Detour via Browning and Derrida." *The Yearbook of English Studies* 39, no. 1/2 (2009): 58–71.

Chinn, Kenneth. "Human Trafficking and Victims of the Sex Trade Industry in California and the Implications for Korea." *Regent Journal of International Law* 10 (2013): 117–130.

Cruz, Lisa. "The Connection between Dissociative Disorder and Sex Trafficking." *Shared Hope International.* Accessed June 20, 2019, www.sharedhope.org/2016/08/connection-dissociative-identity-disorder-sex-trafficking/.

Duran, Nicole. "Who Wants to Marry a Persian King? Gender Games and Wars and the Book of Esther." In *Pregnant Passion: Gender, Sex, and Violence in the Bible.* Cheryl A. Kirk-Duggan, ed. Leiden: Brill, 2004: 71–84.

Farley, Melissa. "Prostitution, Trafficking, and Cultural Amnesia: What We Must Not Know in Order to Keep the Business of Sexual Exploitation Running Smoothly." *Yale Journal of Law & Feminism* 18 (2006): 109–144.

Fox, Michael V. *Character and Ideology in the Book of Esther.* Second Edition. Grand Rapids: William B. Eerdmans Publishing Company, 1991.

Griffin, Gabriele. "Patriarchy." In *A Dictionary of Gender Studies.* Oxford University Press, Accessed April 4, 2019, https://www.oxfordreference.com/view/10.1093/acref/9780191834837.001.0001/acref-9780191834837-e-287?rskey=GuYAhR&result=288

Heath, Elaine. *We Were the Least of These: Reading the Bible with Survivors of Sexual Abuse.* Grand Rapids: Brazos, 2011.

Hodge, D. R. "Sexual Trafficking in the United States: A Domestic Problem with Transnational Dimensions." *Social Work* 53, no. 2 (April 2008):143–152.

"Ishtar." In *Encyclopedia Britannica, Inc.* February 14, 2018. Accessed February 9, 2019, www.britannica.com/topic/Ishtar-Mesopotamian-goddess

Llewellyn-Jones, Lloyd. "Eunuchs and the Royal Harem in Achaemenid Persia (559–331 BC)." In *Eunuchs in Antiquity and Beyond.* Shaun Tougher, and Ra'anan Abusch, eds. London: Classical Press of Wales and Duckworth, 2002: 96–122.

Mapfeka, Tsaurayi K. "Empire and Identity Secrecy: A Postcolonial Reflection on Esther 2:10." In *The Bible, Centres and Margins: Dialogues between Postcolonial African and British Biblical Scholars.* Johanna Stiebert & Musa W. Dube, eds. London: T&T Clark, 2018: 79–95.

Nadar, Sarojini. "'Texts of Terror' – The Conspiracy of Rape in the Bible, Church and Society: The Case of Esther 2: 1–18." In *African Women, Religion, and Health: Essays in Honor of Mercy Amba Ewudziw.* Isabel Apawo Phiri and Sarojini Nadar, eds. Eugene: Wipf and Stock, 2006: 77–95.

Okonofua, Friday, S. Ogbomwan, S. Alutu, O. Kufre and A. Eghosa. "Knowledge, Attitudes, an Experiences of Sex Trafficking by Young Women in Benin City, South-South Nigeria." *Social Science and Medicine* 59 (2004): 1315–1357.

Patterson, Orlando. *Slavery and Social Death: A Comparative Study.* Cambridge: Harvard University Press, 1982.

Reid, Joan. "Entrapment and Enmeshment Schemes Used by Sex Traffickers." *Sexual Abuse* 28, no. 6 (2016): 491–511.

Stern, Craig. "Megillath Esther and the Rule of Law: Disobedience and Obligation." *Rutgers Journal of Law and Religion,* 17 (2015): 244–281.

"The Typology of Modern Slavery: Defining Sex and Labor Trafficking in the United States." Polaris Project. Accessed January 19, 2019, https://polaris-project.org/typology-report.

"Trafficking Terms." *Shared Hope International.* Accessed April 3, 2019, https://sharedhope.org/the-problem/trafficking-terms/.

US Department of State, Trafficking in Persons Report 2014 (Washington, DC: US Department of State Publications, 2014), Accessed December 29, 2019, http://www.state.gov/j/tip/rls/tiprpt/2014/index.htm.

US Department of State, Trafficking in Persons Report June 2018 (Washington, DC: US Department of State Publications, 2018), Accessed March 28, 2020, https://www.state.gov/wp-content/uploads/2019/01/282798.pdf.

Westbrook, Raymond. "Slave and Master in Ancient Near Eastern Law." *Chicago-Kent Law Review* 70, no. 4 (June 1995): 1631–1676.

Willis, Lawrence. "The Depiction of Slavery in the Ancient Novel." *Semeia* 83–84 (1998): 113–132.

Xenophon Cyropaedia 7.5.62–63, translated by Walter Miller. vol. 2. *Harvard University Press,* London and Cambridge, MA: William Heinemann, Ltd., 1914.

2 Sexual trafficking during the Maafa

A site of collective memory for Africana girls and women

In Chapter 1, I outlined parties involved in the process and mechanisms of, and themes and terminologies central to sex trafficking as it is depicted in the book of Esther. In this chapter, I illustrate that the mechanisms of sexual trafficking portrayed in the book of Esther are parallel with the apparatuses of the transatlantic slave trade. Both capitalize on the violent sexual exploitation of Africana females. Attention to this historical cultural trauma elucidates the convergence of ethnic, gender, class, legal, and other oppressions, characteristic of both sexual trafficking and colonial cultures. Further, it illuminates Africa and India as vulnerable geographies where females are targeted and from which they are transported for sexual and labor exploitation. In doing so, I shift the focus from an individual (a Jewish girl, Hadassah) to center a cultural collective (African girls) that exists within a wider collective of ethnically diverse girls and women subjected to the abuse and exploitation of the Persian empire.

Additionally, I highlight that sexual trafficking necessitates the transgression of bodily, spatial, and geographical boundaries and argue that these transgressions are evidenced in the authorized movement of Africana and other minoritized bodies, both in the book of Esther and during the Maafa. This chapter locates sexual trafficking during the Maafa as a site of collective memory for Africana girls and women and delineates how these collective experiences and memories shape many subsequent experiences and relationships of Africana females. Finally, I illustrate how collective memories are tools that provide a link to the past, present, and future, with a specific focus on traumatic experiences and attacks against Africana female bodies and identities. The communication of these collective memories is a form of polyvocality and activism that validates and amplifies minoritized experiences and goes on to challenge and redress injustice.

DOI: 10.4324/9781003168911-3

Collective history: reading the Maafa as a site of cultural traumatization and history for Africana girls and women

Collective memories are communal representations and reconstructions of a group's past that is based on common identity (Licata and Mercy 2015: 194–199). These memories help groups to organize and articulate experiences and memories of the past that impact and are central to the group's cultural, ethnic, national, gender, and/or religious identities. Through cultural memories, groups can identify common themes that are crucial to the formation and sustenance of group identity. This is advantageous because it enables the group to represent perspectives and the particularities of their experiences and traumas from their own viewpoints. Collective memory[1] is, therefore, communal, requiring communication between persons who share similar experiences; it is also fluid and its formation a social initiative. It is the accumulation and articulation of individual and personal histories and memories that are woven together and shaped into collective public memories. Group members communicate not only about *what* they have experienced but also about *how* they have experienced events, and how to best represent those experiences in ways that will preserve their past.

Far too many treatments of the book of Esther focus primarily on the Jewish girl Hadassah and on the Jews' plight even though the narrative reflects the experiences of multiple cultural and ethnic groups. Inasmuch as the story is about its main character, Hadassah, it likewise reflects African girls' experiences as there is an explicit reference to Ethiopia and an implicit reference to girls being gathered and transported to Susa from Ethiopia and other African territories. Many interpretations reflect incomplete and limited perspectives by focusing only on Vashti and Esther's experiences of exploitation, reflecting the interpreter's privilege and/or a lack of a full appreciation for the story's impact on material bodies across the empire or on Africana bodies and identities in contemporary culture. The book of Esther, when read alongside the collective memories and histories of Africana girls and women during the Maafa affords me, an Africana researcher and writer, the opportunity and space to reflect upon their plight as an insider, and to express more experientially how Africana girls and women understand ourselves. I explore how exploitation, displacement, marginality, colonial domination, and other traumatic events impact our identities, histories, and memories as well as our relation to others – in particular, other females and colonial forces. To not apply the lens of intersectionality to the text and historical context and to not read these narratives dialogically renders Africana girls and women invisible and perpetuates further historical, systemic, and cultural oppression. My scholarship is itself an articulation of cultural/collective memory and provides voice and representations of Africana females' experiences of sexual trafficking and trauma. My methodological move, therefore, counters the theoretical invisibility and erasure of Africana girls and women facilitated by single-axis analysis; it affords Africana female bodies visibility and exposes cycles of and silences around sexual trafficking.

Cultural memories of African diasporic girls and women in the Americas center on experiences of enslavement and sexual exploitation during the transatlantic slave trade. The Maafa was a commercial and economic enterprise that lasted approximately four centuries, victimizing African women, men, and children. The conditions were vicious and inhumane. The dehumanization of African peoples was horrifyingly cruel and exploitative, including both physically and sexually. Slave routes included multiple regions and continents, including Africa, the Americas, the Caribbean, Europe, and the Indian Ocean ("Transatlantic Slave Trade"). These locales comprise the circuits in which African labor and sex slaves were moved.

This system of trading and exploitation is the biggest deportation, or forced migration, in history, with millions of Africans being torn from their homes, forcibly moved to unknown and unfamiliar places, subjected to horrendous abuse at every stage. It is estimated that between 25 and 30 million humans were displaced from their native homes, families, and communities, not including those who died on the ships in transit or in the wars or raids connected to capture and trade. Each circuit lasted approximately 18 months. French historian Jean-Michel Deveau emphasizes that the trade and enslavement of African peoples constitutes one of the "greatest tragedies in the history of humanity in terms of scale and duration" ("The Slave Route").

Utilizing the framework applied in the first two chapters, the elements of trafficking and parties involved are as follows: The process entails colonizers recruiting, harboring, transferring, receiving, and displacing millions of African peoples, including girls and women, from their homesteads and homelands. They did so through means of sale, threat, coercion, and abduction for forced labor, enslavement, bondage, sexual exploitation, as well as economic mobilization. Three of the four parties in trafficking systems are not easy to determine because they operated in multiple positions simultaneously. Euro-colonizers, slaveholders, and their male family members: all acted as perpetrators, vendors, *and* facilitators, with many participating in extending the services and capital that made trafficking possible, facilitating and expediting the victimization process, and sexually exploiting the victims. Victims included both Africana children and adult females and males. All were enslaved and trafficked, experiencing sexualized violence and abuse. However, my focus in this book is on the cultural memory and experiences of trafficking Africana females during the Maafa.

African girls and women were multiply burdened and oppressed during the Maafa. They were not only violently and abruptly uprooted and displaced from their communities and separated from their families, including parents, spouses, and children, but they also experienced ferocious organized and non-organized sexual abuse. Vestiges of such practices continue on into the twenty-first century. African girls and women were trafficked along the land and ship routes, and, once ships docked on land, they were further trafficked and sexually exploited by sailors, slaveholders, overseers, and whoever else those with power over them permitted or ordered. Many were impregnated and gave birth in these brutal settings. Political activist and radical legal scholar Angela Davis aptly describes this as sexual terrorism (1981: 39–45). And yet, the sexual exploitation and assault of Africana females was not deemed rape, or criminal, and rationalized as acceptable sexual relations.

Africana female slaves were raped *en masse* – to gratify the sexual desire, depravity, and enactment of power of white slave owners, or as a means for owners or overseers to punish or further humiliate them or their slave husbands. Physical and sexual assaults were often conducted in view of female slaves' chained husbands or brothers who could do nothing to prevent or to protect them from the nefarious attacks (Gay 1999: 5–10). In addition, many African girls and women were subjected to forced breeding to produce children that could contribute to slave owners' economic enterprise. Children born to slaves were often separated from their mothers. In addition, some colonizers gained sexual gratification through inflicting physical pain and mental control, further worsening victims' trauma (Geggus 1996: 265). Sometimes, enslaved raped girls and women were victim-blamed, looked upon with contempt, and further brutalized by slave owners' wives. All these experiences signify profound psychological traumas as Africana girls' and women's humanity and reproductive rights were controlled and denied.

Psychologist Patricia Gay writes of African girls and women's emotional experiences of sexual exploitation during periods of enslavement:

Because their first experience was likely by rape, girls acquired a knowledge of degradation, humiliation, shame, and brutality at an early age. The law protected perpetrators of violence while making it a crime to be virtuous and dangerous to resist. Slave women had to submit to any White man who made advances, at times conceiving the children of sexual predators, and had to make decisions about giving birth to children who were destined to be slaves. Not only could the husband not protect his wife or children from sexual abuse, but also wives, children, and sisters were required to view their men being publicly tortured by castration for minor offenses.

(Gay 1999: 7)

These conditions have similarities with the way sexual abuse is deployed in the book of Esther. Across contexts, colonizers weaponize and use sexual exploitation against Africana girls and women to assert power and domination. Vulnerable enslaved African girls and women like those denoted in the book of Esther are placed in compromising positions and rendered powerless over against their colonial owners. Analogous to how Ahasuerus treats the African virgin girls in the book of Esther, white slave owners exercised power and control over Africana females' bodies and were able to assault them at their discretion. Enslaved African females became sexual victims of white slave owners and traders as part of toxic colonial and patriarchal cultures of abuse. The debasement, degradation, commodification, and exploitation of Africana female bodies are thus a key tenet of slavery and sexual trafficking, which were, and which continue to be facilitated concurrently in both the ancient and more recent contexts.

Similar to what we see in the book of Esther, with no legal protection, Africana girls and women were susceptible to rape and other horrendous conditions that led to grave mental and bodily torture and anguish. Tellingly, during the Maafa, Africana girls and women's living quarters on slave ships were often located below deck near the officers' accommodations, granting officers easy and unrestricted access. This setup echoes the narrative in the book of Esther: colonizing perpetrators of abuse and exploitation ensured that girls and women were in hidden quarters, accessible to abusers, but isolated from persons who could protect them, such as their family members (Rediker 2014: 264.241).

In 2011, at a United Nations Panel Discussion on "Women of African Descent," Verene Shepherd provided an overview of the experiences of

African girls and women who suffered under the European-directed trade of African captives across the Atlantic. Shepherd writes,

> There were four essential lines of historical human trafficking that included women and girls: the internal, domestic trade in Africa; the trade dominated by Western Europeans across the Atlantic, the Arab trade in enslaved Africans across the Sahara to northern Africa and Southern Europe and the Indian Ocean and East African trade towards India. The under-reporting, the destruction of records, the smuggling even after the official ending of the trades, the attempts to downplay the magnitude of the atrocity – all help to explain why it is almost impossible to arrive at any accurate figure of the quantitative dimensions of what is increasingly being called the Maafa or African holocaust. But it was wrong and a crime against humanity, whether it involved 1 or 100 million.
>
> (Shepherd 2011)

In addition to the arduous physical regimes and severe whippings, Shepherd further elucidates how enslaved females were commonly subjected to sexual abuse, writing:

> Neither colonial statutes nor slave codes invested enslaved women with any rights over their own bodies, but rather, transferred and consolidated such rights within the legal person of the enslavers. Male enslavers thus claimed violent access to enslaved women's bodies, and male and female enslavers to their productive labor. Not only did laws not allow the enslaved to refuse these sexual demands made by their enslavers, but they allowed for unrestricted punishment of those who, nevertheless, refused to give in.
>
> (Shepherd 2011)

Shepherd's comments also reveal the centrality of both Africa and India in the transatlantic slave trade. In two separate contexts, Africa and India are geographical locales from which females are targeted, transported, and sexually exploited. This illustrates the geographical scope and scale of the atrocious violence perpetuated against Africana peoples. In addition, the forced movement of ethnic bodies as a means of sexual exploitation characterizes Ethiopia/Africa and India/Asia as vulnerable geographical bodies that house vulnerable material bodies, targeted for capture, transport, and exploitation.

Harriet Jacobs (1813–1897), an African American woman who escaped enslavement and became an abolitionist, in her celebrated autobiography published in 1861, gives a personal account reflecting on the terror that she experienced in the form of persistent sexual harassment and rape by her enslaver:

> But now, I entered on my fifteenth year – a sad epoch in the life of a slave girl. My master began to whisper foul words in my ear. Young as I was, I could not remain ignorant of their import. I tried to treat them with indifference or contempt … But he was my master. I was compelled to live under the same roof with him – where I saw a man forty years my senior daily violating the most sacred commandments of nature. He told me I was his property: that I must be subject to his will in all things.
>
> (Jacobs 2015: 44–55)

Excluded from legal defense and marked for sexual degradation and abuse, no female was exempt from colonial sexual exploitation. Harriet also alludes to collective traumatization by detailing how rape stripped her sister, like other Africana girls, of her childhood. Jacobs writes, "the flowers and sunshine and love were not for her. She drank the cup of sin, and shame and misery, whereof her persecuted race are compelled to drink" (2015: 48). Jacobs's memories of sexual abuse, perpetrated against her and her sister, give a glimpse into how pervasive the issue of sexual enslavement was and how it robbed little Africana girls of their innocence, freedom, peace, dignity, selfhood, and how it challenged their sacrality.

Saartjie Baartman, also known as "the Hottentot Venus," is another example of the commodification and trafficking of Africana girls' and women's bodies. Baartman was a South African woman, born in 1789. Considered one of the first-known Black victims of sexual trafficking, her body was transported, carnivalized, and put on display as an attraction in early nineteenth-century Europe, becoming London's most famous curiosity. Baartman was paraded and made famous for her physique, especially her large buttocks, which were stared at, touched, pinched, stripped, mocked, and admired. In addition, her body became the object of pseudo-scientific and medical "research," which undergirded Eugenics, and many harmful stereotypes and ideas about Black women's sexuality. Even after her death, Baartman's body parts – her sexual organs, brain, and skeleton – remained on display until 1974 (Holmes 2016). Baartman is the tragic figure of the colonized body *par excellence* ("History, Saartje Baartman"). Coupled with sexualized exploitation, her body became souvenir, museum, and "research" project, objectified for consumers' gaze, consumption, and dissection.[2]

Yet another example that illuminates the culture of sexual exploitation during this era is from the diary of British citizen Thomas Thistlewood, who became a slave owner and plantation overseer after migrating to Jamaica. Thistlewood writes about purchasing a young girl named Sally who was aged just 16 in 1762. He records that he raped her 37 times before selling her later that year. On numerous occasions, Sally attempted to escape. In response, Thistlewood would rape Sally again as punishment when she returned or was caught. He also raped Sally as punishment for stealing. He recounts, too, how between raping Sally, he would choose her sexual partners (Hall 1999). These events recounted in Thistlewood's journal in shocking detail, illustrate how routinized sexual exploitation of girls and women was and how central to the enslavement, punishment, and objectification of African peoples. Their bodies became texts that bore repeated and brutal abuse and torture.

Definitions of sexual trafficking reveal an undeniable relationship between sexual trafficking and slavery. Orlando Patterson defines slavery as "the permanent, violent domination of natally alienated and generally dishonored persons" (1982: 13). Patterson's definition underscores that trafficking and enslavement both are exploitative experiences characterized by perpetual violence, shaming, displacement, and domination of subjugated classes, which are determined on grounds of ethnicity/race, social degradation, and/or gender. Sexualized gender-based violence is especially dishonorable and shaming in patriarchal societies that fetishize female sexual purity, such as the society represented in the book of Esther.[3]

Trafficking in every form is starting to be recognized as a practice of modern-day slavery. However, it is important to note that sexual trafficking specifically creates a slave class whereby victims are abducted and/or coerced and subjected to violence and shame just as labor slaves are. Argentinian Supreme Court Justice Carmen Argibay argues that sexual trafficking is a form of enslavement wherein a person exercises power to attach his or her self to the right of ownership of another person's body and sexuality (2003: 375).[4] She writes, "sexual autonomy is a power attaching to the right of ownership of a person, and controlling another person's sexuality is, therefore, a form of slavery" (2003: 375). Therefore, when a perpetrator reduces or minimizes one's sexual autonomy, that perpetrator eradicates a victim's sense of agency and freedom, rendering the subjugated person a sex slave. Sexual slavery is a form of bondage wherein persons are forced into sexual servitude; it is the premeditated raping of persons in brutal and calculated ways. In many cases, there are mass abductions of girls and women for institutionalized and militarized rape.[5]

Trafficking across contexts

Definitions of sexual trafficking and slavery enable readers to recognize how sex trafficking patterns and mechanisms are present in the book of Esther. The Persian colonizer-king uses his political power to recruit, transport, and sexually exploit countless virgin girls. Even after he chooses Esther as his replacement queen, he keeps the other girls, making them his sexual slaves. The force by which he possesses the girls eradicates their freedom and sense of agency; he dominates and minimizes their physical and sexual autonomy. The sexual trafficking of Ethiopian and other African girls in the book of Esther may be imagined as analogous with the experiences of Africana girls and women during the Maafa. Africana female collectives in both ancient and contemporary contexts experienced abduction, transportation to a strange country, erasure of identity, language, customs, and culture, and prolonged exposure to sexualized violence and traumatization with no defense. Sexual trafficking and the transatlantic slave trade are institutional practices that produce(d) collective and traumatic identities: sexual victim and slave. At the intersections of race, ethnicity, nationality, class, and gender oppression, layers of traumatic experiences develop(ed) for Africana girls and women which constitutes historical, cultural, and collective trauma.

The use of sexualized violence as a tool to subjugate and terrorize females is clearly illustrated throughout the first two chapters of Esther. The king and his male officials control Vashti and the entire female collective's sexuality through the creation of a law that enforces and normalizes male supremacy and sexualized violence. Because one male, Memucan, fears, and then projects his fear on to the entire male collective, he suggests the deposition of Vashti, an act of subjugation and erasure. The purpose of her expulsion is to intimidate and terrorize the rest of the females into compliance with male dominance and control. The king approves, and not only obliterates any possibility of gender equality, such as implied by Vashti's concurrent banquet, but legalizes and institutionalizes female subjugation. Vashti and Esther do become insiders in the patriarchal and imperial structures of marriage and nation. The empire's treatment of Vashti, however, is only the beginning of sexual exploitation: brutality escalates when the virgin girls are trafficked into the king's palace. The female collective becomes the subjugated outsider.

In contemporary contexts, girls and women are disproportionately sufferers of the types of violence that are outlined in the book of Esther, because of continuing practices of discrimination and other unjust and prejudicial treatments of persons based on ethnicity, gender, sexual preference, disability, age, and other markers. The United Nations reports on the global pervasiveness and enduring impact of sexual violence against girls and women:

> ...as a manifestation of violence against women, rape and sexual violence, including sexual harassment, are universal, cutting across state borders and cultures, used in all countries and in all cultures as weapons of degradation and terror against women. All forms of sexual violence against women serve as methods of subjugating women by controlling their sexuality through violence, fear, and intimidation.
>
> (The UN Special Rapporteur on Violence Against Women)

Sexual trafficking and other forms of sex exploitation and gender-based violence still today are being used to intimidate and terrorize females. These tactics are used to invoke dread and fear, to scare Africana girls and women back into their "place" as the subordinate sexualized other.

Many scholars have romanticized the book of Esther and the process by which Hadassah becomes queen. However, if we read the narrative utilizing the lenses of intersectionality and collective trauma as our interpretative framework, and with consideration of how African females were exploited through sexual trafficking during the Maafa, we might read the book very differently. In sexual trafficking systems, girls and abusers are linked through boundary flows and movements. That is, sexual trafficking involves flows and travels across national or international borders and is, therefore, a moving epidemic. The flow of sexual trafficking can be bi-directional. In the case of the trafficking of children, there can be a flow of adult offenders across borders to engage in sexual exploitation; or sexual trafficking can include a forced flow of illegally facilitated national or international border crossings by non-consenting and often underage persons. In the story world, instead of the perpetrator traveling to the targets, the virgin girls are brought across geographical boundaries to the king's palace, a privilege that stems from his colonial and imperial power. Flow and movement are ordered by the king and simultaneously legalized by his imperial edict (2:8). During the Maafa, imperial perpetrators both traveled to various locales, abusing girls and women in those geographical environments, and trafficked the abducted and wounded females to new milieus wherein they were subjected to yet more sexual exploitation, physical abuse, separation from family and kin, and erasure of culture, among other traumatizing experiences.

This reveals how movement and boundaries play significant roles in sexual trafficking. Sexual trafficking is predicated on the transgression of sexual boundaries, most often initiated through the transgression of spatial boundaries. In the book of Esther, the frequent movement serves to isolate and prevent Hadassah and the other virgin girls from making connections with each other and the king's other wives and concubines who are sequestered elsewhere in his palace. This, surely, is aimed at obstructing any attempts of resistance. The girls are, indeed, in continuous movement from the time that they are taken from their homes and home provinces until right after Esther is chosen as queen. Movement in Esther takes place in two steps. First, the girls are taken from their homes within their provinces and transported across geographical boundaries to the king's palace. Second, once inside the palace complex, they are taken across other, internal spatial boundaries and transferred between harems and the king's bedroom. During transit, bodily and sexual boundaries are transgressed as well.

To understand such transgressions requires a refusal to focus merely on spatial and geographical borders. We must attend to bodily incursions as well. Anthropologist Vania Smith-Oak and biochemist and molecular geneticist Megan Marshalla explain the relationship between intersectional identity, power, exploitation, and bodily boundary transgressions in their research. Smith-Oak and Marshalla note that bodies connect with other bodies across multiple boundaries: physical boundaries of the skin, social boundaries of ethnicity, class, and gender, and sensory boundaries between bodies (2019: 114). Bodies therefore become useful instruments for understanding the reproduction of inequalities as they connect or create distance, cross boundaries, as allowed through social scripts, and have the capacity to either damage or heal other bodies. Bodies are not only objects but are also central to the creation of knowledge and the housing of knowledge; consequently, they are sites for intellectual inquiry (2019: 114).

Smith-Oak and Marshalla note that the bodies of persons occupying the highest positions in social hierarchies are afforded certain privileges to transgress the bodily boundaries of those lower on the social hierarchy. For example, in the book of Esther, Persian males occupy the highest positions in the social hierarchy established by their colonizing society and culture and, consequently, have power and privileges to transgress the bodies of colonized ethnic female bodies of lower social standing. Similarly, European males that occupied the highest positions in the social hierarchy during the Maafa transgressed the bodies of Africana females and women, who as female, Africana, and enslaved, occupied the lowest social positions.

Oak and Marshalla further maintain that interactions between bodies and the boundaries crossed, produce a knowledge that reveals troubling perspectives and practices, while at the same time blurring other boundaries between those with and those without agency and power (2019: 115). The depiction of the sexual interaction between the body of the king and the bodies of African and other minoritized girls, and the legalization of this non-consensual bodily boundary crossing, promotes the ideology that African and other minoritized girls are rapable, do not deserve protection, and that the boundaries of minoritized females are transgressable and not theirs to control. Not only is this knowledge produced, but it is also dispersed in the form of edicts and sent (in everyone's own script and language) throughout the king's provinces, ensuring all know of his authorization to cross spatial/geographical/sexual boundaries, which, in turn, destabilizes the girls' physical bodily boundaries and integrities.

In the biblical text, the king's rank and power afford him the privilege to control the girls' bodies. His male agential body crosses various boundaries in ways that map and reproduce bodily and social differences and injustices and reinforce the gendered social hierarchy set up in the first chapter. This boundary-transgressing process exposes how certain bodies with a constellation of identifications, specifically African female bodies, are viewed and treated by society due to their ethnicity/race/social standing. These practices have strong resonance with practices of Euro-colonizers during the Maafa. In both contexts, female bodies that are acted upon are constructed as socially and economically vulnerable and, subsequently, as disenfranchised (Smith-Oak and Marshalla 2019: 115). Because they are all female, ethnically minoritized, and impoverished, they are viewed by those with privilege and power as having no, few, or permeable and breachable boundaries. There are few, if any, social regulations attached to their vulnerable bodies (Smith-Oak and Marshalla 2019: 122).

Attention to these types of boundary crossings unveils various troubling frameworks, structures, ideologies, principles, and values of the societies that enable the exploitation and abuse of vulnerable bodies (Smith-Oak and Marshalla 2019: 122). Those numerous girls are rounded up and transported to the king's palace without apparent resistance reflects the powerlessness of the girls and of their families to repel the authority and power of the king. The manifestation of social inequalities and hierarchies that lend support to these types of bodily transgressions provides a sobering reminder of the ties between colonialism and sexual violence, especially the types of violence enacted against Africana females during the Maafa.

Across contexts, seeing and being seen, touching and being touched, are conditioned in particular ways by those involved in the sexual trafficking economy (Smith-Oak and Marshalla 2019: 115). In the book of Esther, the king selects his new queen in a form of display, gathering the girls after sending edicts across his provinces. The written edicts provide all the people in the empire with access to the knowledge that the girls are being taken into the palace; the recipients can see the edicts and the girls being gathered and transported. The actions of sexual trafficking are thus public, as well as common and communal knowledge. Moreover, the king conditions the people in his provinces to accept his orders of sexualized violence when he legalizes the trafficking process. Trafficking of the virgin girls follows Vashti's public deposition for refusing to be objectified through voyeurism. Each time a female – Vashti or one of the virgin girls – is seen or hidden from others' view, it is because the king orders it. Male fixation on minoritized bodies is central to the story, as evidenced already in the king's collection (a veritable catalog of girls from *every* province in the realm, 2:3) of these vulnerable, foreign/ethnic bodies as his royal property. Once in the palace, in a guarded fortress (2:3), the girls are separated not only from their families and communities but also made invisible to all outsiders (with the sole exception of Esther who can communicate with Mordecai). Then, after the second chapter, they are completely elided from the narrative.

During the process of sexual trafficking, the virgin girls are touched by the king at his discretion. The narrator reveals that each night a girl goes in to the king, a euphemism that obscures the sexual exploitation, but does not go back into his bedroom unless he delights in her and calls her by name (2:14). One can imagine the traumatic revulsion at being lined up for selection. These actions serve as social cues to the girls that seeing and being seen, touching and being touched, are dictated by the king and by those he appoints. For example, Hegai directs and conditions Hadassah on how to be touched in ways that will enable her to advance with the king (2:15). She obeys Hegai and wins the king's favor, and ultimately the royal crown (2:17). The female collective is therefore conditioned to be seen and touched by men, when men order it. Such sexualized sociopolitical process of boundary crossing reveals the hierarchical position of colonial and patriarchal males in determining boundaries and regulating how these are crossed.

In this process, the king and his officials legislate migration: they control and facilitate how and when the girls enter Susa; set the criteria for their entry (beautiful, young, virgins, female, from the king's provinces); facilitate travel; establish guidelines for a beautification process that commences once the girls are transported to and secluded in the king's palace; and determine that the girls will remain in Susa indefinitely where they become sexual slaves of the king after Esther is chosen as queen to replace Vashti. These decrees legalize sex trafficking, enabling the king not only to facilitate the smuggling of African and other ethnic bodies across national boundaries but also to transgress all other personal and bodily boundaries when he forces the girls to have sex with him. He does this to assert his imperial authority and to concretize patriarchy after both are threatened by Vashti's resistance. The imperial presence embodied by the king and his officials in this story is intrusive and disruptive, sanctioning the exploitative treatment of vulnerable girls, and constructing a reality marked by multiple traumas: namely, traumas of displacement, objectification, sexual exploitation, and enslavement. Recognizing this process as it unfolds within the narrative further exposes the inherent violence and horror of this biblical text. The similarities between the practices of colonizers and the abuse of African females in both the text and contemporary contexts are undeniable.

The girls in the text are uncovered, touched, and violated when the king penetrates their bodies, exploring their "anatomical geographies," exposing the hidden terrain under their clothes and skin (Smith-Oak and Marshalla 2019: 115). His touch is horrific, unacceptable. The king's boundary crossing violates physical, sexual, personal, and social boundaries in ways that disrupt the girls' sense of identity and safety. His actions suggest that neither their bodies nor their boundaries matter. Such somatic transactions not only reflect social inequalities but also lead to psychological symptoms, including fragmentation, guilt, self-doubt, inability to establish other interpersonal relationships, and disassociation, which provides a way to escape or to attempt to handle the overwhelming fear and pain. On multiple levels, such abuse is damaging, distressing, and wrong.

In patriarchal and colonial societies, such as the one reflected in the book of Esther, bodies are not only valued for their labor-potential but virginity is also an asset that increases a female's economic value. In essence, because the king gathers countless virgin bodies and brings those vulnerable displaced bodies to his palace, he gains capital. Each evening, a girl goes and is raped by the king, and in the morning, she is dismissed to go to the second harem of the concubines. The girls, no longer virgins, lose economic value and are sent to holding cells in the event that the king wishes to call one or another back to his bedroom. Michael Fox argues that these holding cells of the harems are a form of imprisonment: oppressively regulated atmospheres with a regimen preparing the girls for another's pleasure (1991: 35). A girl does not have a chance to go back in to the king, unless he "delights" in her and calls her back "by name." The implication is that these girls have no worth in the eye of the king, unless they prove themselves "good at" having sex with him (1991: 35).

Bringing the virgin girls to Susa also serves other strategic interests by further disenfranchising the people of the king's provinces. On top of the obvious physical and emotional exploitation, sexual exploitation is an exploitation of a region's resources and capital. This observation is not to reduce the girls' value to their virginity status and sexuality. Their lives and bodies are, however, valuable to their communities in other, including economic, ways, such as for forging bonds and alliances between families. The king recognizes their capital potential and seizes it for himself to destabilize their natal communities. In the contemporary context, a common reason cited by those who support the continuation of sexual trafficking is that sexual trafficking leads to wealth creation and economic gains for those who have few opportunities (Bryant-Davis et al. 2009: 72). In ancient and contemporary colonial contexts, though, the bulk of gains and wealth rarely go to the victim or even her family. Both may receive some compensation, but colonizers usually find ways to minimize any benefit that could be accrued, taking the biggest share for themselves.

I understand African girls' and women's lives, bodies, and histories as sacred texts with the capacity to provide information and inspiration. Their lives and experiences are worthy of exploration, investigation, and interpretation. When we are attentive to the movement of female bodies in the ancient context, it becomes clearer that national, home, and bodily borders are transgressed when the girls are transported from their native provinces to Susa, from their homes to the king's palace, and from one harem to the king's bedroom, to another harem. Similarly, when we are attentive to the bodies of those transported and abused during the Maafa, we become keenly aware that not only geographical boundaries were crossed, but also bodily and sexual boundaries of Africana girls and women were transgressed. Collective memories and histories of Africana girls and women clarify that movement of bodies and boundary infractions are mechanisms in sexual trafficking enterprises past and up to the present. These mechanisms, moreover, cause past and ongoing traumatization among Africana females right up to the present.

An intersectional framework, moreover, emphasizes the convergence of ethnic, gender, and class identities that contribute to increased vulnerability to trafficking. The racialized minoritized bodies of Esther and the collective memories of the Maafa of Africana females bear witness to the many transgressions that have left indelible physical and psychological scars. Yet, collective memories afford Africana females opportunities to articulate the specificities of their traumatization from their own perspective, to make meaning of these experiences, and to resist contestation and negotiation of their identities and personhoods.

Collective memory: collective resistance to sexual trafficking and history silencing

Trauma is broadly defined as either an experience or an enduring condition that is overwhelmingly stressful and inhibits an individual's ability to cope. Psychologists assert that it is the subjective experience of objective events that constitutes trauma. In other words, the more one believes they are endangered by conditions, the more traumatized that person becomes. Moreover, trauma manifests in various forms, and traumatic effects are often cumulative. Clinical psychologist, victimologist, and traumatologist Yael Danieli asserts that multigenerational transmission of trauma is an integral part of human history, often transmitted orally, or through writings, in stories, songs, in body language, and even in silences (1998: 1). Sadly, far too many marginalized and subjugated peoples bear witness to multigenerational trauma in their written and oral testimonies of lived experiences. Consider, for example, diasporic enslaved Africans in colonial territories, Native Americans in a land conquered and exploited by colonizers, survivors of the Jewish Shoah (or Holocaust), sexually exploited Korean "comfort women," to name only a few.[6]

Because Africana girls and women are one minoritized and objectified group disproportionately represented among victims of sexual trafficking, they, too, experience what Orlando Patterson (1998) has termed cultural trauma. Cultural trauma is characterized and caused not only by collective and intergenerational exploitation but also by a threat to and loss of personhood and cultural identity. When members of the Africana female collective were made sexual slaves, they lost physical, personal, and sexual autonomy. In addition, white slave masters forced them to learn new languages and to appropriate European customs, religion, and culture.

Psychologists Thema Bryant-Davis, Hecwoon Chung, and Shaquita Tillman affirm the psychological impact of intergenerational cultural injustices against Africana females in their research, "From the Margins to the Center: Ethnic Minority Women and the Mental Health Effects of Sexual Assault" (2009). They stress that the trauma of sexual assault is intensified for many ethnic women due to the interlocking experiences of such societal traumas as racism, sexism, and poverty. In other words, the socio-historical context of intergenerational trauma in the lives of ethnic minorities is and remains a part of the contemporary experience of sexualized violence (2009: 330).

According to Orlando Patterson, sexual trafficking and the exploitation of children constitute modern forms of slavery with social, economic, cultural, and psychological consequences. The resulting effects of this cultural, intergenerational trauma manifest into what scholar and activist Randall Robinson terms a "spirit injury" that leads to the loss of self-esteem, pride, and sense of belonging. He argues that the collective's whole memory is crushed under the remorseless commerce of slavery (2001: 11–14, 26–28). In addition, the United States' perpetuation of racialized myths and social stigmas continues to depict Africana people as people without worth or history. The suffering of Africana females during the Maafa has become the inherited suffering of present-day African diasporic girls and women. Many contemporary Africana females, unfortunately, endure experiences of sexualized trauma into the twenty-first century replicating injustices done to their brutalized ancestors. Racialized and gendered social hierarchies, ideologies, and stereotypes, and discrimination continue to impact Africana culture and souls, both in the United States and elsewhere.

Patricia Gay adds that the descendants of enslaved and sexually exploited African women continue to live with the psychological consequences of institutionalized sexual violence. She emphasizes that sexual violence against Africana females is not a singular occurrence that happened at a specific point in time but that it began with slavery, continued through subsequent generations, and persists up to the present in various forms of sexual and other trauma (Gay 1995: 5). Gay, furthermore, comments on initiating the healing process, affirming the group's sense of its collective self, and engaging in collective remembrance, as follows,

Slavery included sexual trauma that has been institutionalized and, thus, continues to injure African American women.
The trauma is dealt with in the African and African American
spiritual tradition of testifying to, and witnessing of, our history
and experience. Though continuing to struggle with the psychological consequences of racism, the collective testimony and
witness combined with social action is self-affirming and the beginning of healing.

(Gay 1995: 5)

Whereas subsequent-generation victims of sexual trafficking are differentiated from first-generation victims, recognizing, and naming the
cultural memories of sexual trafficking experienced by the Africana
female collective allows members of the collective, after centuries of
depersonalization, dehumanization, and marginalization, to be per-
sonalized and humanized. Historically, certain subjects and institutions have had political control over the narration of slave and sexual
trafficking stories and of how sexual exploitation is depicted in those
stories. Therefore, a feature of cultural memory is for the impacted
group to relate and preserve knowledge themselves. This aims to
redress how perpetrators and their descendants controlled the representation process[7] and further perpetuated what many scholars term
"the conspiracy of silence" against victims of trauma. This seizure of
the narrative has constituted yet another mode of depersonalization
for victims. Moreover, perpetrators also generated more traumatic
violence by silencing and "gas lighting" groups trying to process profoundly complex and layered memories of sexualized violence. This
has been exacerbated, too, by widespread reactions from members of
the public, such as reactions of indifference, avoidance, repression,
denial, and victim-blaming. Narratives deemed "too horrifying to believe" often result in reactions of disbelief or denial, as well as in the
myth and perception that victims and survivors actively or passively
participated in their own suffering (Danieli 1998: 4).

Africana females need an agency of their own collective memories,
since it is they who embody the painful experiences and memories
of sexualized violence. The collective memories and histories *about*
the sexual enslavement of Africana females *by* dominant cultures ignore crucial details about the experience of sexualized violence and
signify how the act of collective remembering can be a highly racialized process. This process is steered by cultural elites who, wittingly
or not, produce knowledge that marginalizes, re-victimizes, or erases
traumatic events, thereby upholding colonial agendas, ideologies,

and myths. Institutions and cultural groups with power and privilege downplay the experiences and insights of marginalized groups and often focus on their construction of successes, such as on material and economic features. What is sidelined and made invisible is the impact of trafficking and enslavement on material Africana bodies. Collective memory formation and the cherishing of the collective memory of the trafficked, the enslaved and their descendants is one way to acknowledge the traumatic impact of and to challenge past *and* contemporary forms of sexual trafficking and slavery. It is also one important way to confront racism and ethnic-gender-class-based sexual oppression.

Although white colonizers attempted to wipe away the cultural knowledge, consciousness, and histories of those captured and sexually abused, the sexual exploitations of Africana females have become institutionalized memories of culture that have been collected, transmitted, and reincorporated throughout the generations. These stories not only showcase the many instances of sexualized violence against Africana girls and women but also recount how some were able to circumvent oppressive structures to survive and advocate for protections against such vile acts. These actions of resistance and resilience prove that those who experience sexual trafficking are more than victims; they are survivors and abolitionists.

The creation of collective memories is highly significant for Africana peoples because during periods of British colonization, Africana people were not afforded opportunities to include their collective memories in texts, or to express them through formal rites or celebrations. Such denied experiences are another aspect of the cultural and collective trauma that Africana peoples endured, the suppression of their histories and memories by dominant cultural collectives. Collective memories enable the Africana female collective to express the painful experiences of colonial government-sanctioned sexual enslavement. Such memories not only produce knowledge but also document the pervasive issue of sexual trafficking, break the stigma, shame, and silence that have enabled trafficking to thrive, and confront cultural amnesia.

Harnessing collective memories enables Africana girls and women to challenge ideologies, critique stereotypes and exploitative and abusive practices such as the process, means, and goals of trafficking, and to share the stories of those whose lives have been marked by such abuse, both in biblical texts like the book of Esther and in their own lives. Moreover, the collective memories of Africana females help members of other collectives, including abusers and descendants of abusers, to grapple with moral convictions and their own understandings of power, privilege, abuse, and the role of sacred texts in embodiments of each.

All these features of collective memory are connected to and an expansion of the work that is facilitated by the #SayHerName movement. According to the movement's co-founder, Kimberlé Crenshaw, collective memories produced by the #SayHerName movement enable us to include and share the names and stories of Africana females that are generally missing from America's collective memories of systemic racism and police brutality; and, to raise awareness about the impact of systemic racism and legal injustices upon Africana girls and women.[8] The #SayHerName movement exposes the role of intersectional oppression in violence against Africana females and does so across global platforms which increases its scope and impact. The framework of intersectionality, which is central to the #SayHerName movement, illustrates that Africana girls' and women's social identities, such as ethnicity, gender, and class identities are mutually constitutive and contribute to discrimination against, injury, and deaths of Africana females, internationally. Moreover, as a source of polyvocality, the #SayHerName movement further unmasks and challenges the various ways and reasons that Africana females experience sexualized and other physical abuse and oppression, including dominant voices and interpretations of biblical texts and history continuing to silence and render Africana girls and women invisible.

Although cultural memories are distinguished by distance (often of centuries) between originating events and the present, the historical struggles and traumas of Africana females are alive in the treatment of Africana girls and women in contexts today. One legacy of past abuse is that it is linked to modern-day experiences of extreme discrimination and sexualized traumatization; therefore, cultural memory has distance from, yet resonates in the present. Evoked in the present, collective memory refers to the past and expresses hope for transformation in the future. As such, collective memory connects all three temporal dimensions. Collective memory is not merely fixated on the past but is a necessary foundation for both majority and minority groups looking to more promising futures, especially by preventing catastrophes and traumatic events resulting from experiences in the past.

When Africana girls' and women's experiences and stories are read and reflected upon intertextually, both within the book of Esther and the narratives of enslavement and suffering during the Maafa and on into the twenty-first century, we are left with a succession of narratives of sexualized violence that shout out loudly and indignantly about the undisputable damage done to the integrity, dignity, and humanity of

Africana female bodies, psyches, and spirits. These girls and women, past and present, were and continue to be ripped from their families, isolated, and then violated. Their wills are ignored, leaving their pain to intensify. Their stories reflect and articulate the unconscionable and brutal abuses perpetrated by colonial and neocolonial powers against Africana women and girls. Through collective memory, members of the collective can connect, collaborate, and communicate through time and in the present to produce a shared framework of reference that shaped and that continues to shape identity. This process enables Africana women to create community and solidarity.

This chapter specifically, and the book more widely, is an act of recalling and localizing collective memories of Africana girls and women that center sexual trafficking and enslavement. They are collective memories of abuse and exploitation and of traumatization and fragmentation. As such, this book contributes to and expands the #SayHerName movement by clarifying tormenting historical truths: patriarchs and colonial rulers had explicit sexual access to colonized, minoritized, and racialized girls and women that had no legal protections and that these (his)stories, when read intertextually produces a deep historical picture of the nexus of trafficking, enslavement, ethnicity, sexuality, law, and religion. Yet, as expressions of collective memories, these articulations resist sexualized violence and narrative silencing and have the potential to transform societies by galvanizing members of different and wider collectives to challenge oppressive and detrimental actions that negatively impact Africana females and their collective identity.

In this chapter, I identify the sexual trafficking of Africana girls and women during the Maafa as an instance of collective trauma and site of collective memory. The collective memories of Africana girls and women are organized and articulated memories of centuries-long systematic physical and sexual abuse at the hands of colonizers. Through collective memory, this group articulates the impact of sexualized traumatic experiences on Africana females' identities and formation, identifying perpetrators of exploitation and abuse, and classifying geographical spaces as sites of immense cruelty and violence. Additionally, I illustrated that the collective memory of the Maafa, when read alongside the biblical narrative that describes how African girls were sexually trafficked and exploited by a Persian king, further enables the group to reconstruct a past that is based on common experiences and identities. Finally, this chapter uncovered that collective memory also has the potential to transform societies and communities by galvanizing members both within and outside of the collective to challenge oppressive and violent actions that deteriorate collective identity.

Notes

1 "Cultural memory" is a form of collective memory that is shared by a cultural community, or group within it. I use the wider term "collective memory" here and throughout this book, because I analyze and/or refer to multiple collectives in my research on Esther. I analyze females as a collective, males as a collective, African females as a collective, the eunuchs as a collective, the Jews as a collective, the Persians as a collective, etc. All these identified collectives belong to different groups with sometimes overlapping yet distinct cultural identities, histories, and memories. Intersectionality and polyvocality afford opportunities to assess the particularity of the experiences of multiple cultural collectives and the impact of these experiences on the cultural collectives' identities through cultural memory.

2 See Harvey Young, *Embodying Black Experience: Stillness, Critical Memory, and the Black Body* (Ann Harbor: University of Michigan Press, 2010); Rosemary Wiss, "Lipreading: Remembering Saartjie Baartman," in *The Australian Journal of Anthropology* Vol. 5, no. 3 (1994): 11–40. For a visual of a female Hottentot, please see image at Wellcome Collection site: https://wellcomecollection.org/works/ajwtbghx.

3 This high valuation of purity is underscored particularly by the narrator's repeated references to the virginity of the girls gathered for the king's sexual pleasure.

4 See also, Angella Son, "Inadequate Innocence of Korean Comfort Girls-Women: Obliterated Dignity and Shamed Self," in *Pastoral Psychology* Vol. 67 (2018): 175–194; Yoshimi Yoshiaki, *Comfort Women: Sexual Slavery in the Japanese Military during World War II* (New York: Columbia University Press, 2000).

5 Another term for sexual slavery is servile marriage. Sexual slavery is a universal problem and manifests differently in different contexts. To cite several diverse examples: Korean "comfort women" exploited by Japanese invaders, Ghanaian trokosi, Indian sati, and the sexual enslavement imposed by Islamic State on Yazidi women of Iraq.

6 Angella Son created the term *"comfort girls-women"* to replace the traditional, wider used term of "comfort women." Son's use of "comfort" signifies the sexual enslavement of the victims; the inclusion of "girl," underscores the young ages of the victims; and the use of "women" reflects the long period of time that the victims endured without any satisfactory resolution of their situation – let alone justice. See "Inadequate Innocence of Korean Comfort Girls-Women: Obliterated Dignity and Shamed Self," in *Pastoral Psychology* Vol. 67 (2018): 175–194.

7 Joy DeGruy refers to this process as "un-sanitizing history." See Joy DeGruy, *Post Traumatic Slave Syndrome* (Portland: Joy DeGruy Publications, Inc., 2005).

8 Mary Louise Kelly, host speaks to Kimberlé Crenshaw, Co-Founder of #SayHerName, "'Say Her Name': How the Fight For Racial Justice Can

Be More Inclusive of Black Women," America Reckons with Racial Injustice, NPR (podcast) July 7, 2020, Accessed July 7, 2021, https://www.npr.org/transcripts/888498009

Works Cited

Argibay, Carmen. "Sexual Slavery and the 'Comfort Women' of World War II." *Berkeley Journal of International Law* 21 (2003): 375–389.

Bryant-Davis, Thema, Heewoon Chung, and Shaquita Tillman. "From the Margins to the Center: Ethnic Minority Women and the Mental Health Effects of Sexual Assault." *Trauma, Violence, & Abuse* 10, no. 4 (2009): 330–357.

Bryant-Davis, Thema, Shaquita Tillman, Alison Marks, and Kimberly Smith. "Millennium Abolitionists: Addressing the Sexual Trafficking of African Women." *Beliefs and Values* 1, no. 1 (2009): 69–78.

Danieli, Yael, ed. *International Handbook of Multigenerational Legacies of Trauma*. New York: Springer, 1998.

Davis, Angela. "Rape, Racism, and the Capitalistic Setting." *The Black Scholar* 12, no. 6 (November/December 1981): 39–45.

Gay, Patricia. "Slavery as Sexual Atrocity." *Sexual Addition & Compulsivity* 6, no. 1 (1999): 5–10.

Geggus, David. "Slave and Free Colored Women in Saint Domingue." In *More than Chattel: Black Women and Slavery in the Americas.* David Gaspar and Darlene Clark Hine, eds. Bloomington: Indiana University Press, 1996: 259–277.

Hall, Douglas. *In Miserable Slavery: Thomas Thistlewood in Jamaica, 1750–86*. Barbados, Jamaica, Trinidad and Tobago: The University of West Indies Press, 1999.

"History, Saartje Baartman, The Hottentot Venus: The Figure of the Colonized Body," The Funambulist. Accessed April 20, 2019, https://thefunambulist.net/cinema/history-saartjie-baartman-the-hottentot-venus-the-figure-of-the-colonized-body.

Holmes, Rachel. *The Hottentot Venus: The Life and Death of Saartjie Baartman: Born 1789–Buried 2002*. London: Bloomsbury 2016.

Jacobs, Harriett. *Incidents in the Life of a Slave Girl.* Oxford: Oxford University Press, 2015.

Licata, Laurent and Aurelie Mercy. "Social Psychology of Collective Memory." In *International Encyclopedia of the Social & Behavioral Sciences.* 2nd Edition. James D. Wright, ed. Oxford, UK: Elsevier, Vol. 4, (2015):194–199.

Patterson, Orlando. *Slavery and Social Death: A Comparative Study.* Cambridge, MA and London: Harvard University Press, 1982.

Rediker, Marcus. *The Slave Ship: A Human History.* New York: Penguin Books, 2014.

Robinson, Randall. *The Debt: What America Owes to Blacks.* New York: Penguin, 2001.

Shepherd, Verene. "Women, the Transatlantic Trade in Captured Africans and Enslavement: An Overview." Panel Discussion on "Women of African Descent," IYPAD, United Nations, New York: October 19, 2011. Accessed https://www.ohchr.org/Documents/Issues/Racism/WGEAPD/Women-VerenePresentation.doc.

Smith-Oak, Vania and Megan K. Marshalla. "Crossing Bodily, Social, and Intimate Boundaries: How Class, Ethnic, and Gender Differences Are Reproduced in Medical Training in Mexico." *American Anthropologist* 121, no. 1 (2019): 113–125.

"The Slave Route." UNESCO. Accessed July 24, 2019, http://www.unesco.org/new/en/social-and-human-sciences/themes/slave-route/transatlantic-slave-trade/

"Transatlantic Slave Trade." United Nations Educational, Scientific and Cultural Organization. Accessed July 7, 2019, http://www.unesco.org/new/en/social-and-human-sciences/themes/slave-route/transatlantic-slave-trade/.

UN Commission on Human Rights. *Report of the Special Rapporteur on Violence against Women, Its Causes and Consequences, Radhika Coomaraswamy.* February 12, 1997, E/CN.4/1997/47. Accessed March 16, 2021, https://www.refworld.org/docid/3b00f4104.html.

3 Stereotypes and social and cultural attitudes regarding the Africana female collective and how these attitudes contribute to sexual violence

In this chapter, I discuss stereotypes and social and cultural attitudes about Africana female identity and sexuality and how these ideologies and attitudes contribute to sexual violence both in contemporary contexts and within the book of Esther. I also identify textual and interpretative cover-ups, which inhibit readers' and interpreters' ability to perceive the objectification, oppression, exploitation, commodification, and traumatization of African girls in the text. Euphemisms mask issues of gender and sexuality and soften the presentation of the sexual and gender-based abuse in the text. Finally, I discuss the application of the genre of comedy to the book of Esther and some implications of this hermeneutical framing.

Further, I suggest that readers apply instead the genre of horror because it better prepares readers for the gruesome sexualized violence, affords a more serious framework that enables readers to unmask, identify, and critique social and cultural attitudes regarding Africana female identity, and brings the intersectional oppression, trauma, and social injustices against the African female collective to the fore. The horror genre also elucidates that stereotyping is another form of violence endured by Africana girls and women and is often exacerbated by challenges to sexual trafficking research, which double as a "cover-up" by enabling sexual trafficking to flourish with little to no legal consequence for perpetrators and facilitators.

Stereotyping and cultural attitudes: a precursor to sex trafficking

The previous chapters demonstrated that Africana girls and women are among victims of multiple forms of violence at the hands of patriarchs and colonizers in the book of Esther as well as during the Maafa. Further, women, girls, and those perceived as "other" on account of

DOI: 10.4324/9781003168911-4

their ethnicity, sexual preference, gender identity, (dis)ability, among other markers of difference, as well as those who are "othered" on multiple or intersectional counts, are especially prone to suffering sexualized violence, including sexual trafficking. I provided definitions of sex trafficking, identified the three elements of trafficking (process, means, and goal), as well as the parties involved in trafficking in both the literary and historical contexts. In doing so, I revealed that in both contexts, colonizers transgressed geographical, bodily, and sexual boundaries of Africana girls and women who were intentionally targeted, gathered, dislocated, and sexually exploited. Both the king and other colonizers violently asserted superiority, repressed difference, enforced dependence, and, through practices of discrimination and physical and sexual exploitation, instituted social and cultural attitudes that have encouraged bias and caused significant and ongoing harm.

According to Kimberlé Crenshaw, a unique benefit of intersectionality is that it can expose and critique the stereotypes and ideologies, sex-based norms, and laws that implicitly and explicitly justify the maltreatment of Africana girls and women (1989: 155–159). It is therefore imperative to consider the ways that marginalized racialized groups experience intersectional forms of discrimination, oppression, and violence. This hermeneutic underscores that intersectional forms of oppression are systemic, multidimensional, and are linked to practices of power and the struggles for power. Further, this type of analysis elucidates that institutionalized power structures are responsible for constructing gender norms and practices and for delineating the boundaries for gendered subjects, which, in turn, create opportunities for abuses of power through sexual trafficking.

Sexualized violence is often justified or undergirded by stereotypes about Africana females' sexuality. For example, during the Maafa, not only were Africana girls and women reduced to the status of chattel, considered subhuman, and differentiated from other peoples to justify their enslavement but, many colonizers also claimed that they were sexually exotic, lewd, and aggressive, which contributed to their eroticization and abuse (Bravo 2012: 1–38). Stereotypes used to justify the sexual exploitation of Africana females, which originated during times of slavery and continue to manifest up until the present, have been well researched and documented. Some pervasive images include Africana females as promiscuous, seductive, hypersexual, loose, whorish, lustful, and immoral.[1] These stereotypes, alongside the absence of legal recourse or access to help for raped and otherwise sexually exploited Africana girls and women, undergird the ideology, dominant for much of US history, that Africana females were and are "unrapable" – because rape presupposes human integrity and the ability to consent. Carole Christensen who is a psychologist, sex therapist, and pioneer in cross-cultural and anti-racist studies notes the paradox: "the only women to ever suffer socially sanctioned and induced sexual abuse were branded 'loose and immoral'" (Christensen 1988: 192). Racist stereotypes such as these continue to exacerbate the tragedy of sexual trafficking and increase victims' vulnerability to it.

The "Jezebel myth," to give one example of a prominent racist stereotype, is modeled on biblical Jezebel who (against any evidence recorded in scripture) came to be mischaracterized as a figure of lust, sexual impurity, and wickedness, also as Black. The Black, lascivious Jezebel stands in contrast to the white, pure Virgin Mary. And, this pervasive stereotype has served over centuries to frame Africana females as "other," sexually loose, morally suspect, provocative, and seductive (Butler 2015a: 127). Sociologist Patricia Hill Collins (2000) reports, too, that the Jezebel image provided a powerful inversion and rationalization for the sexual atrocities perpetuated *against* enslaved African women. By branding Africana women as "Jezebel" and sexual temptresses, *they* became the evil ones, responsible for tempting men, as opposed to what they actually were: namely, victims of male sexual aggression.

Mammy is another stereotypical figure. As a Black servant (or, better, slave), Mammy performed domestic and childcaring duties for her master with little or no financial compensation. Emphasis is placed on her work, strength, and caretaking, which reinforces that Africana females are strong, capable (if simple), and happily seeking multiple servile roles – as opposed to assuming them out of necessity. The Mammy image is associated with the matriarch stereotype, which symbolizes strength, self-sufficiency, forbearance, and resilience, all characteristics that can be associated with a culture of silence (Tillman et al. 2010: 63–64). These images present Africana females as self-sacrificing, able to withstand anything, and as willing to selflessly meet the needs of all (white) others (West 1995: 459–461).

Another emphasis is on her physical features which influenced Africana females' beauty regimes and eating patterns. The overweight mammy figure, especially when compared to the white families that she serves, is a desexualized and peripheral domestic worker wearing unstylish and unassuming apparel. She is caricatured as submissive, nurturing, loyal, and utterly and willingly dependent. Although she is visible, she lacks interiority, the ability to fully exercise agency, and the capacity to challenge the conditions and contexts in which she finds herself. As such, she is often depicted as both harmless and humorous. While the Jezebel figure is oversexualized, some of her features are somewhat in line with seductive white feminine beauty standards of early American history (a small frame and waist, curved hips, fairer skin). This is in contrast to the asexual, dark-skinned, overweight mammy figure with her large breasts and buttocks. In the twenty-first century, meanwhile, large breasts and buttocks, alongside full lips and darker skin tones are considered one desirable beauty standard. This look is so popular that girls and women of various ethnicities are paying large sums of money to undergo cosmetic surgery and tanning, alongside applying new make-up techniques, to achieve these beauty ideals.

Last, Sapphire is a hostile, nagging, iron-willed woman, the precursor of the "Mad Black Woman" of modern comedy stereotype. Sapphire is depicted as gratuitously assertive, even scary, and as treacherous toward Black men. This stereotype and its display of emasculation of Black men made the Sapphire figure comical and appealing to white audiences – in part by playing to and assuaging white fears of Black men. It also problematizes expressions of anger and rage, both of which can be experienced in response to sexual traumatization. The stereotype is employed to trivialize or condemn expressions of Black emotionality, including expressions that might help victims process traumatization (West 1995: 461–462).

These social myths purport that Africana females have either an insatiable appetite for loose sex and embody an emasculating brashness or have Mammy-like passivity and unquestioning devotion to white domestic concerns (Harris-Perry 2013: 50). In both cases, these stereotypes and myths designate Africana girls and women as sexual deviants and targets of sexual abuse (Butler 2015b: 1471). In addition, pornographic depictions of Africana bodies show racialized violence and torture as forms of erotica. Bryant-Davis and Pratyusha Tummala-Narra emphasize,

> Racialized stereotypes of sexual availability, immorality, promiscuity and animalism, and eroticism based on pain and subjugation, and a belief that some subgroups of women and girls exist for the purpose of men's sexual pleasure and/or domination over them have informed the creation of pornography, promoted objectification, and proscribed sexual roles of ethnically diverse women.
>
> (2017: 155)

Cheryl Nelson Butler, professor of Law and Legal Studies, adds that stereotypes reflect a culture of "racialized gender," or oppression based upon the intersection of race and gender. She notes that children of color are generally stereotyped as sexually aggressive, deviant, and predisposed toward risky behavior. In addition, Black children are often stereotyped as dysfunctional misfits whose inherently sexually promiscuous nature undermines the moral standards of (white) mainstream society. Butler concludes that the perceived hypersexuality of both teens and women of color is regarded as a social threat that contributes to their sexual exploitation (2015b: 1485).

Expanding the work of social anthropologist Fredrik Barth, Hebrew Bible scholar Linda Stargel asserts that social categorization is a necessary component of collective identity, as it allows collectives to form and maintain boundaries or boundary markers, by grouping together similar people, objects, and events. In doing so, groups represent "us" and "them" so as to distinguish between group members and non-group members. Categories that help to define identity and mark boundaries include race, ethnicity, gender, sex, sexuality, citizenship, or non-citizenship status, all of which can make persons more or less vulnerable to systemic violence, exploitation, and oppression (2018: 3–6). This process of categorization and representation also leads to hypervisibility of the "other," and to the creation and projection of stereotypes by one group on to another. Simultaneously, the dominant group has the power to blur the identities of the "other" subordinate group.

We see this boundary demarcation happening in multiple ways in both the literary and historical contexts that I examine. In both contexts, colonial forces and their provinces (the domains where they exert power) are marked; perpetrators and those trafficked are distinguished; and geographical boundaries are marked and crossed. For example, the socio-political structure of the United States was heavily influenced by its "founding" fathers' understandings of their own religious identity as "Christian," and their foundation of a "Christian" nation. This "Christianity" has also been ingrained and sustained by ideologies of racial superiority and gender stratification, as well as of genocide, enslavement, cultural disenfranchisement, sexual abuse, and exploitation. This has also contributed to institutional racism, sexism, classism, and an inequitable social stratification, whereby many persons injured through the means of trafficking are disenfranchised and traumatized. Analogously, genealogical data and narrative clues distinguish "the Jews" from "the Persians" and "the Amalekites" in the book of Esther. Social stratification in both ancient and contemporary contexts categorizes persons based on race/ethnicity, gender, and power, which has historically positioned whites/other colonial subjects at the top of the hierarchy and Africana and other minoritized persons at the bottom.

Let me digress to focus on the ethnic group called the Amalekites. As recorded in scripture, the Amalekites had a long-standing and consistently negative relationship with the Jews. They are descended from Amalek, one of the sons of Esau (Gen 36:12) and first attack the Hebrews while they are wandering in the wilderness (Exod 17:8–15). In fact, in the Torah, there are two commandments regarding Amalek: to obliterate the nation and to never forget their deeds (Deut 25:17–19). Later, in I Samuel 15, Saul is commanded by Samuel to obliterate Amalek. Saul is successful in battle but chooses to spare the Amalekite king, Agag. Although Samuel eventually kills Agag, Saul's failure to completely obliterate Amalek costs him the kingship. In addition, Agag bore a son before he was killed, and Haman is a descendant of Agag's son and rises up once more as the villain in Jewish history and tradition. The Amalekites, therefore, are a notorious and maligned ethnic group, the archetypal enemy of the Jews that represent and stereotype the worst form of evil. As such, they are perpetually slated for destruction. Though the book of Esther centers on the tensions between Haman and Mordecai, the Jews and the Amalekites, I have suggested we widen our lens to also focus on the unprovoked and unsettling sexualized attack on the virgin girls of various ethnic groups. Perhaps Esther's deployment of violence is a trauma response not only to the threat against the Jews but also to experiences of sexualized violence (both as an individual and as part of a collective). The king orders Haman to be hanged on the gallows he had built for Mordecai after Haman throws himself on the couch where Queen Esther was reclining (7:8). This account suggests that the king perceives Haman's actions as a sexualized attack on Esther. Ironically, he fails to acknowledge his own sexually exploitative and violent actions.[2] The nameless faceless virgin girls, however, have been mostly blotted out of our memories. This is the type of erasure that #MeToo and #SayHerName critique and challenge. I, too, reorient attention to these girls in the story world, to give voice to their stories and to keep their memories alive, even though we don't know their names. We should not be comfortable with the sexualized violence perpetuated against girls or women in the text or in our contemporary contexts, nor with narrative, oral, or historical practices that blot out their memories. These are no laughing matters. Sexual trafficking, like other forms of gender-based violence, is a serious matter that deserves serious attention.

Returning to Stargel, she further maintains that categorization is moderated by the use of stereotyping, which emphasizes similarities between units of a particular category – people, events, concepts, etc. – while minimizing difference (2018: 6). These differences can be real or imagined, not shared by all, most, or any of the collective. Stereotypes are often shared to reflect one's group's perception of the other group. For example, in the book of Esther, Haman's statement about "the Jews" is an example of stereotyping:

> There is a certain people scattered and separated among the peo-ples in all the provinces of your kingdom; their laws are different from those of every other people, and they do not keep the king's laws, so that it is not appropriate for the king to tolerate them.
>
> (3:8)

Haman's claim is not supported with any detail, let alone any evidence. His statement contains some truth: the Jews *are* a scattered people with distinctive customs. But the truth is twisted to make distinctive-ness subversive: without elaboration on Jewish laws, these are cast as *ipso facto* constituting disobedience to the king's laws. Moreover, this vague claim becomes legitimation for not tolerating Jews. In this way, the stereotype Haman asserts results in imminent threat to the "cer-tain people's" safety and livelihood, when he goes on to petition for the king to issue a decree to facilitate their destruction (3:9) – which is granted (3:10).

The use of "certain" identifies the Jews as a dubious ethnic other. Na-tividad Chong notes that the dominant discourse refers to "ethnicity" as belonging to an other and inferior culture because the reproduction of features of identity, such as indigenous languages, native origin, ru-ral origin, ethnic ancestry, and the safeguard of native cultures are of-ten depicted as markers of underdevelopment or backwardness (2014: 197). Not only are ethnic others cast as inferior, but often as exotic as well. Political and cultural sociologist Joane Nagel explains that with regard to ethnic minority women, this includes sexually exotic dimensions, because it lends itself, within a heteronormative and het-erosexual frame, to give men the illusion of experiencing the "exotic," constructed as a sexual adventure, or conquest. Consequently, Nagel speaks of "ethnosexual frontiers," which she describes as "the bor-derlands on either side of ethnic divides; they skirt the edges of ethnic communities; they constitute symbolic and physical sensual spaces where sexual imaginings and sexual contact occur between members of different racial, ethnic and national groups" (2003: 14). These, in turn, become volatile social spaces, fertile sites for the eruption of vi-olence (2003: 56).

Nagel's conceptualization of ethnosexual frontiers builds on Ed-ward Said's analysis of Orientalism and the stereotypes of the East/ Orient held by the West/Occident. Said traces the development of these perceptions back to the colonial periods of British and European domination, and concludes that Europeans claimed that people of "the Orient" were inferior to Europeans (if compelling on account of their "exoticism") and required domination. European colonizers perceived the Orient as not only exotic and foreign but also erotic and irrational. These stereotypical images and understandings of the Orient justified all of physical domination, sexual objectification, and exploitation the Eastern other.[3]

Sociologist Mimi Sheller provides a further example of ethnosexual frontiers with reference to sex-trafficking enterprises. Hence, Sheller underscores how the Caribbean – to give one example – is branded and marketed as tropical playground or erotic paradise, a place for sex tourists seeking to experience "exotic peoples." Sheller points out that Jamaica has been cast as an ideal place for sexual tourism and trafficking, in part through its landscape, which includes "verdant forests, exotic flora, and tropical greenery," all signifying "Eden" or other primitive garden spaces, or "virgin forests," in the imagination of its visitors. Sheller contends that such depictions of the Caribbean "lent support to the institution of slavery by celebrating its capacity to make wildlands productive" (2004: 24). She argues further that "naturalization" of the social and economic inequalities of the contemporary tourist economy occurred in three steps: objectification of Caribbean people as part of the natural landscape, the equation of that landscape with sexuality and corruption, and the marketing of the Caribbean via imagined geographies of tropical enticement and sexual ability.[4] As a result, the sexualization of exotic brown bodies has become a standard tool of Caribbean tourist promotion and feeds into the development and sustainment of sexual tourism and trafficking in the region.[5]

Hiddenness and concealment of victims' identity also intersect with stereotypes to disenfranchise and oppress them. The narrator of Esther fails to mention explicitly the ethnicities of the virgin girls, disclosing only the bracketing provinces of the king's geographical dominion. But there are no genealogical references for Vashti or the virgin girls, nor are their native origins or mother tongues named. The narrative and ideological effect of the omission of these details is the erasure of ancestral and ethnic roots and the presentation of these vulnerable ethnic girls as inferior and exposed to sexual trafficking.

Stereotypes not only contribute to the creation and shaping of identity but also influence the ways Africana females understand themselves and how they relate to others. Many girls grow up to believe that a heightened sexual persona is central to their sexual identity as Africana girls (Butler 2015b: 1487). Bryant-Davis et al. maintain that silence and stereotypes are simultaneous weapons used against Africana girls and women (2009: 331). They delineate the impact of stereotypes in the following way: "Cultural beliefs that devalue women while making them responsible for male sexual behavior and cultural beliefs that honor the silent sacrifice of the self for the assumed honor of the family or community can be devastating or detrimental" (2009: 339). Additionally, Bryant-Davis and Tummala-Narra further postulate that stereotypes are created and perpetuated to feed into the desire and justification for persons to purchase and exploit racially and ethnically marginalized persons. Therefore, the racial and ethnic stereotypes that describe ethnic minorities as animalistic, facilitate objectification and dehumanization. which precede other discriminatory and exploitative acts (2017: 154). The consequences of these stereotypes are that they endorse racism and sexism while at the same time promoting socially reinforced cognitive distortions, specifically about women of a particular cultural group (2017: 154–155).

Ethicist Traci C. West's work illustrates the relationship between stereotypes and violence against Africana women in the twenty-first century. In "A Moral Epistemology of Gender Violence," West writes about the ties between communal moral knowledge and the endangerment of Black women. She notes that lawmakers and representatives of religious institutions and community resources – community members that are in positions *to protect, serve, and/or grant other resources to Black female victim-survivors of violence* – make crucial judgments about whether Black girls and women are "deserving" and have "moral worth." Many of these community members are informed by damaging attitudes to Black racial identity, preconceived moral assumptions, and prejudicial notions as to behavioral norms regarding Black women. These attitudes frequently lead to a reluctance to respond to reports of violence against Black women, as well as to other behaviors that endanger them. West cites as an example the failure of police to prioritize investigating reports of violence made by Black women and/or their families. Additionally, writing about the intersections of religion and violence against Black women, West underscores that some clergy members reinforce morally distorted understandings of marital obligation and sex/gender norms. For example, the assertion of clergy and religious leaders that "good Black women" or "good Black Christian women" are faithful to their husbands and endure spousal abuse. West urges representatives of these institutions and activist groups to investigate and challenge the competing and demeaning moral truths attached to poor Black women's racial identities, to ensure the safety of women disproportionately impacted by violence (2012: 171–186).

Oppressive images, stereotypes, and ideologies have traumatic implications for the identity formation of Africana females. For one, that which is imagined and projected upon ethnic minorities produces real, material consequences for them. The normalized transgression of bodily and sexual boundaries depicted in the book of Esther, I argue, impacts on and contributes to the formation of collective identity for Jewish, Africana, and other minoritized females. By failing to address their experiences as constitutive of abuse and traumatization, interpreters, albeit inadvertently, uphold ideologies that Africana girls and women cannot be violated. This ideology is rooted in notions that persons of African descent are not fully human, that the crime of the rape of Africana girls and women is non-existent, and that they do not deserve protection from oppression. If it is not recognized, in its blatant and in its subtler forms, it cannot be resisted.

Sexual trafficking, similar to and compounded by slavery, has in the past and continues to impact the cultural collective identity of African diasporic females. This collective identity is intricately connected to and impacted by collective memories and histories of endemic sexual assaults. The psychological presence of trauma negatively impacts Africana men, women, and children, and continues to impact emerging generations in unhealthy and psychologically harmful ways. One aim of this book is to resist the stereotypes and ideologies that have been used to justify the abuse of Africana females. In doing so, I am re-mapping and re-narrating the environment from a suppressed yet contextual, candid, creative, passionate, particular, and powerful position that opens the world to the realities, struggles, and strivings of a resilient and culturally persistent collective. After all, context shapes not only *what* we read but also *how* we read. In the following section, I identify ideological claims and stereotypes and assess embodiments of difference that undergird and justify the sexual exploitation of African females in the biblical text.

Euphemisms and cover-ups

There are several problems related to gender and sexuality within the book of Esther that deserve attention. According to Randall Bailey, one problem is that there are sexual issues embedded within the book, especially around the "sexual beauty contest" to replace Queen Vashti. Another is that the sexual exploitation in the biblical text is so horrific that we have been conditioned not to see its presence. Bailey argues that on the one hand, the practice of sexual exploitation is so horrific that rather than being bothered by its presence, we develop a reading strategy of "not seeing what is there." On the other hand, personal biases and opinions have led translators to cover up meanings of words to conceal the presence of sexual acts or references (2009: 234). Similarly, Sarojini Nadar implicates contemporary interpreters, whom she calls out as co-conspirators in this "cover-up," because of their "brushing off" of rape (2006: 88). Fox asserts these cover-ups by modern interpreters are an injustice to girls all over the world who are currently being abused and exploited and are used as toys in the sexual games of the powerful (1991: 36). For example, when we cover up or ignore the abuse in the text, we continue to forfeit justice for those exploited by Jeffery Epstein, Robert Craft, Bill Cosby, Robert Kelly, and other girls and women that are targeted exploited by gangs and terrorist groups globally. We delay justice for many girls and women who are forced into trafficking and tourism and for those whose experiences are brought to the fore by the #MeToo and #SayHerName movements.

Because of focus on such terms as "beautiful" and "cosmetic treatments," many scholars have dismissed or overlooked sexual trafficking in the book. Hadassah and countless virgin girls are taken to the king's harem not merely to be beautified but to be forced into sex. To disguise this requires extra glamorization, which emphasizes aesthetic and sexual appeal before the girls are swept into the king's bedroom. Volition and consent are not part of the process, Instead, the empire confiscates and violates these girls' beautiful bodies. The beautification process and soft euphemistic rhetoric conceal the objectification and commodification of the girls. It destigmatizes the exploitation and removes or minimizes hints of sexual violence. The physical, sexual, and psychological violence impressed upon the girls communicates that they are utterly worthless except for exploitation by the king. The use of euphemisms, distractions, and cover-ups masks the cruelty of sexual trafficking as humorous or sexy and consequently negates the injuries done to the girls.

As a weapon of colonial control, sexual trafficking thrives on victims' silence, invisibility, and heightened vulnerability. The silence surrounding sexual trafficking and the hyper-invisibility of victims is pervasive, diminishing victims' agency and allowing trafficking economies to flourish. Yet silence can still be very disruptive. If only we would listen to the quiet screams, the hushed pleas and petitions to "see me, hear me, protect me, advocate for me!" Attention to the silences in both biblical texts and contemporary contexts can and should disrupt normative modes of interpretation, illuminating the psychological trauma that has gone unvoiced and suppressed for far too long.

There are troubling silences in the book of Esther and in the history of its interpretations. There are things not stated by the narrator, details suppressed through the use of euphemisms, and characters' voices that are simply not heard. For example, many interpreters choose to focus primarily on the main character, Esther, for whom the book is named, further rendering invisible and silent the other girls gathered and exploited by the king (2:2–4; 2:19). Interpreters fail to notice the intersecting ethnic, gender, and social locations of the virgin girls; the details of capture, displacement, and sexual trafficking; and the girls' silenced voices. The absence of these girls' voices erases the physical harm and psychological suffering that they must have endured. They are not allowed to protest their sufferings, nor do their male guardians get the opportunity to protest these girls' exploitation. The silencing of protest by the narrator is equally horrifying. Yet, if we pay attention to the words *not* spoken in the book of Esther, we can see that the silences throughout this narrative present soundless shrieks and inaudible stutters of throbbing hostility, paralyzing trauma, and terror.

In addition to silence, secrecy is a prominent theme in Esther 2. Hadassah's guardian Mordecai forbids her from revealing her ethnicity and family background when she is taken into the royal harem, raising questions about the role that he plays in her exploitation and oppression. Indeed, the identities and names of the numerous other virgin girls brought to the king's harem are likewise concealed by the narrator. Euphemisms used to describe actions that the virgin girls are forced to take, such as "the girl who pleases the king" or "with whom the king delights," have further contributed to this silence and secrecy, obscuring the sexual abuse and trauma embedded in the text. Similar to how we see sexual trafficking operating as an "invisible" institution in the text, perpetrators, vendors, and facilitators of sexualized violence and abuse in contemporary contexts depend on, profit from, and thrive on silence, suppressed voices, secrecy, obscure laws, and underreporting of abuse. These parties weaponize victims' silence and fear, using it to perpetuate abduction, transportation, and sexual exploitation, particularly of Africana girls and women across national and international borders. This process is illustrated in both the narrative world of Esther and in contemporary sexual trafficking discourse.

Traci West addresses these issues in a more recent context. In her seminal work, *Wounds of the Spirit: Black Women, Violence and Resistance,* West critiques the misnaming of rape as "consensual sex," due to generalizations and assumptions that legitimate violence: the assertion that women are liars and their testimonies unreliable; women are in need of or desire Black male assaults; and, violence at the hands of males is passionate, romantic, and a response to sexual allure (1999: 122–150). These false claims – which West describes as destructive gender and race cultural cues (5) – serve as "cover-ups" for the ideologies, cultural conditions, and dynamics that lead to and keep male violence against Africana girls and women secure in modern settings. These assumptions are analogous to ideas that justify methods utilized by modern-day sex traffickers.

West notes that the trauma experience, cultural messages, and other often hidden communal and institutional barriers, such as access to programs and public shaming, may cause or contribute to fear and silence among contemporary victim-survivors of intimate and sexualized violence (1999: 138). Sometimes, women may resort to silence and use shame as a form of resistance and survival (1999: 165). However, West writes that speaking out can constitute a social change on behalf of Black females and demonstrates a resistance strategy to violence perpetrated against them (1999: 178–179).

Last, West notes that when Black women reflect on their assault, they do so struggling between resisting and absorbing the cultural meanings attached to that assault experience and their trauma is deepened by the diverse deprecating cultural messages that overwhelm them (1999: 122). Like Dr. West, I am committed to amplifying the experiences and vantage points of Africana girls and women, to breaking silences and transforming shame around sexual assault and violence, and to persistently challenging the cultural scripts about our worth and dignity, so that we can collectively work toward resistance and healings.

Foregrounding and framing cultural stories, such as those of the Maafa, and analyzing these stories dialogically with biblical texts such as the book of Esther, allows cultural collectives to represent their trauma while bridging the past with the present, and do so from their "own site, apart from the demands, the gaze and authority of whites."[6] This type of hermeneutic enables Africana females, in particular, to shift back and forth between the past and the present, making connections between texts and contexts and identifying analogous ideologies, rhetoric, stereotypes, and practices that are mirrored in both societies and cultures.

From humor to horror: interpreting Esther as a horror story

In Esther discourse, recurrently highlighted themes, genres, and phrases guide and direct readers to see certain aspects of the text and to neglect others. Indeed, multiple genres have been assigned to the story, including historical narrative, Persian court chronicle, diaspora novel, hero's tale, romance tale, and carnival tale. But, as I have argued already, much more is needed to fully explore the intersectionalities and polyvocality of the text, because these can orient the reader's focus to other elements of the text that identify and reveal exploitation and trauma. We should note that Esther and Mordecai are mobilized as the narrative unfolds to prevent the attempted genocide of the Jews. But no one is mobilized to rescue the victims of sexual exploitation, the many girls and women in the story world, whose abuse is not just threatened but carried out and then diminished, glossed over.

Deploying the genre of carnivalesque, biblical scholar Bruce Jones maintains that

> readers should not object to the way in which women are treated in the book because to do so would be to miss that the objectionable features of the book are deliberate absurdities which the author has used skillfully.... The author is not praising the Persian Court but laughing at it.
>
> (1982: 437)

Such a reading, however, misses the representation and seriousness of sexual trafficking by choosing to focus on humor, farce, exaggeration, and other literary devices that completely fail to critique the violence of empire and patriarchy. Reading the book as a diaspora novel, meanwhile, trivializes the story and encourages readers to focus on plot elements such as survival and identity negotiation in a diasporic context. But again, this fails to expose sexual trafficking as a widespread trauma endured disproportionately by vulnerable and marginalized minorities, such as the Jewish people in this story world and also the other colonized peoples of the empire. Many readers have also skipped over the presence of trafficking in the text, due to the use of downplaying terms such as "beautiful," and "cosmetic treatments," which may explain why some interpret the organized sexual violation of multiple girls in terms of pageantry. Euphemisms such as "the girls who please the king," or in whom the king "delights," further mask the sexual abuse and trauma embedded in the text.

Yet another reason readers miss the portrayal of sexual trafficking in the book of Esther, is because they tend to focus on individual incidents of violence. Except for the Jews as a collective, there is a tendency to assess and focus on the book's major characters (Mordecai, Ahasuerus, Esther, Haman) and on a single incident of threatened violence

(Haman's plot to exterminate the Jews), rather than to reflect on other (if more minor) characters and on violence against other gendered and ethnic collectives (the virgin girls, the eunuchs, the Amalekites, those slaughtered on the streets of Susa). These factors obscure sexual trafficking and other acts of violence in the book of Esther.

Humor and the comic mode are prominent themes in Esther scholarship. Scholars note multiple anachronisms, exaggerations, inaccuracies, and hyperboles throughout the narrative and comment on how the story is rife with dramatic reversals and inversions of power. For example, biblical scholar Adele Berlin refers to the book as "comic entertainment" (2001: 2–14). Creative writer and publisher Celina Spiegel suggests that there is a carnival spirit throughout the book of Esther that critiques the Persian government, its representatives, and laws, and envisions a world remade (1994: 202). Similarly, Kathleen O'Connor observes that the book of Esther is downright hilarious but in a very serious way. Noting ironies, grotesque exaggerations, and sharp turnabouts, she argues that Esther's humor is at the expense of the Persians and functions as "a work of political satire, a survival tactic and an act of hope" (2003: 52–53).[7] O'Connor posits that ironic reversals of situations and exaggerations function specifically to shame and humiliate Haman in particular, and the Persian government more generally. For example, Haman expects and demands honor from Mordecai, and has a hugely proportioned gallows erected for him, which becomes the gallows upon which he is hanged. O'Connor also claims that other violence within the book is exaggerated, constituting a feature of the tragicomic genre of the book, and representing reversals of fortune. The violence within the book, therefore, "telegraphs the plot reversals as the weak overcomes the strong and the humble put down the arrogant" (2003: 55).

O'Connor further reflects on the mockery of the king and the government, noting that Ahasuerus is incapable of thinking or making any decisions for himself. His actions and all his royal decisions are prompted and directed by other characters: his officials, eunuchs, Haman, Esther, and Mordecai. Focusing on Esther, she writes that more than once Esther manipulates the "royal buffoon." For,

> to survive within a system of domination requires calculation, manipulation and trickery. These are highly developed skills of people with no other way to affect the course of events. They are the diplomatic strategies of any people with no power and one of the strategies at which women have excelled. They are not to be scorned.

These are tactics that Esther has to use to subvert what O'Connor calls "immovable power" (2003: 58). O'Connor concludes that humor functions as a political weapon, an act of survival and a scathing critique of the Persian Empire and all of its constituents, turning situations upside down, reversing expectations and situations, which, she argues, implies an open future for the Jews and promises life on the other side of sorrow and pain (2003: 62–64). However, O'Connor's analysis again ignores the sexual exploitation of virgin girls. She does not mention their abuse or the danger they are in – only that of the Jews.

Nicole Duran claims that the dismissal of the book's explicit foray into gender politics interests her for two reasons: first, it effectively silences a certain discussion of the text's political implications and second, it reflects the cultural rootedness of interpretation that any portrayal of men as actively asserting their supremacy is read as humorous. She notes that historically, "any prominent woman showing evidence of being able to function without a man is still considered threatening not only to patriarchal but also to family and social structures" (2004: 74). This may be why Vashti is deposed.[8] Notably, Duran rejects the role of humor and laughter and claims that both humor and laughter mute and subvert gender politics (2004: 74) and, might I add, the stories of Vashti's replacement and of the abuse of the virgin girls in particular.

Humor can hold a serious role in postcolonialism, as it creates the space for marginalized and minoritized voices to raise critiques and rebellion against colonial forces and their legacies. But humor also often reinforces the colonialist values being resisted. In addition, those who employ humor often write in ways that cause characters to conform to imperial values, as we see played out in the book of Esther. Written in a diasporic context to critique and challenge the Persian Empire, the story's two major characters, Esther and Mordecai, not only coopt power to resist the empire's oppressive regime but also gain prominent positions within it and enact violence against other groups, just as the empire had enacted violence on them. They are grafted into the official state that they endeavor to overturn. But instead of mocking or rejecting the dominant culture, they mimic its violence and oppressiveness, a result of internalized oppression.

Writers utilizing humor often mock that which is ridiculous and/or exaggerated. They tend not, however, to recognize the sexual trafficking depicted in the book of Esther, or to appreciate it as such. It is all too often sidelined or overlooked altogether. The trafficking of the young virgin girls is not identified or called out as humorous, nor is it perceived as ridiculous, ugly, vile, senseless, or as an act of exploitation and human rights violation on the part of the king and Persian

Empire. The capture and captivity of countless beautiful girls by traffickers might seem an exaggerated detail of the biblical narrative – but this type of widespread abuse is prevalent up until today. For instance, since 1987 the Lord's Resistance Army, which has Christian roots and has operated above all in Uganda under the leadership of Joseph Kony, has actively carried out atrocities including mass abductions and child sex slavery. And since 2013, Boko Haram, an extremist Islamist group, has seized over a thousand boys and girls in Nigeria. Many of the girls were imprisoned and abused while the boys were put to work as fighters. In 2014, 276 girls were taken from their school in Chibok, which sparked international outrage and the #BringBackOurGirls social media campaign. Although some managed to escape, Haram leaders imprisoned, enslaved, raped, and impregnated many of the girls, forcing some to marry fighters in its camps.[9] Just recently in 2021, even as many nations wrestled to combat the deadly Covid-19 pandemic, another scourge continued: gangs and bandits were unrelenting in carrying out mass abductions in Nigeria.[10] This story of contemporary cultural trauma along with the Esther narrative reflects damage to the integrity of Africana female bodies and spirits and articulates horror: all of the victims experienced kidnap, being held hostage (by either rebel groups or colonial powers), and were exposed to brutal, and, in some cases, fatal violence.

Interpreting this narrative through the lens of humor, many readers focus attention on the threat of the violent killing of the Jews and on the frenzied killing of their enemies, not on the violent and systematic sexual assaults on the African and other virgin girls. There are other social-political issues at play at the center of this story, namely how the empire constructs its identity around patriarchy, a gendered hierarchy, and extensive sexual exploitation. This construction of identity and its by-products are in no way laughable or humorous not least because their toxic power remains destructive up into the present.

If readers do not identify sexual trafficking in the narrative, how then can this systemic structure and oppression be critiqued and disrupted? We must start considering the psychological impact of not only colonialism but also the convergence of colonialism, patriarchy, and sexual trafficking of Africana girls and women. Examining the convergence of these traumatic experiences illuminates how gender is constructed and policed in colonial settings and how patriarchal cultures contribute to female marginalization and exploitation and thereby support rape and trafficking cultures.

In her documentary, *Toni Morrison: The Pieces I Am* (2019), American novelist and professor Toni Morrison reflects on growing up in the

1940s and 1950s and on her experience of encountering Black girls in books. She recounts, "in every book I read about young Black girls... they were props, jokes, topsy... no one took them serious ever." This tradition of perceiving Africana girls and women's lives and experiences as funny and not taking acts of oppression and violence against them seriously, is why I use my interpreter's privilege to assess the biblical text, utilizing a more serious framework of biblical horror. Because the narrative is one that describes and details gendered violence, exploitation, terror, and horror, I suggest the book of Esther should be considered as belonging to a genre of biblical horror. By reading the book of Esther as horror, we are made sharply aware of social injustices and violations of human rights in ancient and contemporary contexts. Reading the book of Esther through the lens of the horror genre highlights this trauma further, by encouraging readers to name and confront the wounds of both individuals and collectives that are widely ignored and suppressed in both sacred and cultural narratives. Identifying the horrific language and imagery in the text challenges us to confront the patriarchal and colonial causes of sexual trafficking, and to recognize the impact of such violence on collective identities, histories, and memories. This recognition and confrontation are a necessary first step to active resistance and the dismantling of trafficking structures and the mechanisms that support or mask them.

The word "horror" comes from Latin *horrere/orur* and French *orror,* both meaning "to tremble" or "to shudder." In English, "horror" is defined as intense feelings of fear, shock, disgust, or dismay ("Horror") Recently, biblical scholars have begun to analyze how biblical literature reflects the language, concepts, imagery, and storylines of the horror genre, such as reflected in contemporary horror films. Although many films that reflect biblical stories shed light on obsessive or extreme violence, such as the violent acts in the Noah narrative, the killings and plagues during the exodus, and the brutal death of Jesus,[11] much of the scholarship on the Bible and horror focuses on how the Bible is featured in and impacts on contemporary horror films.[12] In this section, I do not wish to consider horror as it is depicted or alluded to in films based on the biblical story. Rather, I am highlighting the horrific details presented in the book of Esther as a means of highlighting the outrageous violence perpetrated against the female collective in the narrative world.

Horror as genre enables readers to become more attentive to the gruesome and cruel processes, practices, structures, and ideologies of sexual trafficking in the book of Esther. There is nothing funny about sexual abuse and exploitation. Although interpreters may recognize humor, farce, exaggerations, and other literary devices for critiquing the empire and patriarchal power structures within the narrative, placing this biblical book within the genre of biblical horror can help to identify an even more potent form of violence and exploitation that the story grapples with: namely, large-scale sexual trafficking as mass trauma that almost all the female characters of the story endure (Esther, Vashti, and the virgin girls from India to Ethiopia). (One exception is Zeresh.) Moreover, we are made to think further about gender roles and how having female and feminized bodies (including here the eunuchs) often predisposes to extreme violence and despicable pain. If this is not recognized and acknowledged in the text, it is more easily hidden elsewhere, too. If this is not appreciated in its horror, how can it be resisted?

The horror genre presents terror and horrifying violence in ways that evoke physical, physiological, and psychological responses from its audiences. It often reflects contemporary social anxieties, focusing on that which is considered dangerous, fearsome, or repulsive. According to Tina Pippin, feminist scholar of religious and gender studies, horror has an uncanny (German *unheimlich*) edge, presenting what is familiar to us in unfamiliar ways that incite feelings of dread and fear (2002: 80).[13] Pippin asserts that horror allows us to express our worst fears and possibly hopes in literary form so that we can share our anxieties with others (2002: 79). Moreover, through horror, "present fears and oppressions are visible in the vivid descriptions of the monstrous and its destruction" (2002: 80). Read as horror, the book of Esther thus reveals and exposes the unsettling yet familiar phenomenon of sexual trafficking in an unfamiliar way, leaving some readers disturbed and uncomfortable.

Biblical and feminist scholar Amy Kalmanofsky defines biblical horror as a "composite emotional response to a threatening entity or situation comprising the emotions of fear and shame" (2008: 75). She identifies two distinct perspectives of biblical horror: *direct horror,* which is the emotional response to a dangerous and threatening entity, such as an encroaching enemy, and *indirect horror,* the emotional response to the impact of the threatening entity's work. Both induce fear and shame (2008: 75). According to Kalmanofsky, in cases of direct horror, the threatening entity provokes both the fear of becoming a victim and the shame of weakness and defeat (2008: 75–76).

We see this process at work in the book of Esther. The virgin girls endured exploitation and abuse at the hands of the Persian Empire. Not only does the king encroach upon the girls' bodies but the empire also induces fear by separating the girls from their families, before preparing them for sexual abuse, and by continued isolation from families and communities once Esther is chosen to replace Vashti as queen. While details of their emotional response to being displaced and raped are lacking, readers know that in patriarchal societies, girls and women are valued and esteemed for their chastity. Therefore, losing their "virgin" status subjects the girls and their families to societal shame. Sexual exploitation is thus not only a tool to evoke fear in the girls but also to scare and disenfranchise their families. The latter is also a means of minimizing resistance to imperial rule. As with the deposition of Vashti and the subsequent law to gather and collect virgin girls for the king's sexual pleasure, "the devastated serve as terrifying reminders for the observers of their own vulnerability and as warnings that they too could suffer a shameful fate" (Kalmanofsky 2008: 76).

As well as provoking fear and shame, another key feature of the horror genre is the presence of repeated, outrageous violence enacted on or by abject, gendered bodies (Graybill 2017: 50). As I have already illustrated, the book of Esther is layered with violence, which serves to provoke both fear and shame in the female collective. The violence is perpetrated against the abject and horrified bodies of young Africana girls, as they are transported, incarcerated, and raped. After each girl has had non-consensual sexual intercourse with the king, she is taken back to another harem – a type of "holding cell" – until such a time as the king calls her back again "by name" (Fox 1991: 35). Like Vashti, they appear to be expendable, serving the interests of the empire. Thus, Vashti and the virgin girls become the personification of abject horror, as well as the characters in this story through whom we, the audience, experience our own sense of horror.[14]

Despite, or perhaps because of, female bodies being abject objects of horror in Esther, the narrator seems to be obsessed with them. As so often in the context of horror films, outrageous violence is perpetrated against multiple women and girls, demonstrating the interchangeability of female bodies (Graybill 2017: 51). Moreover, in the first two chapters of the book, these bodies are "opened" in more than one way: they are "opened" to the gaze of others (the king, his noblemen, and servants) and are subsequently forcefully, sexually "opened" by the king when he rapes them. Opened female bodies thus become entirely interchangeable in this process. Initially, it is Vashti's body that the king seeks to "open" for the consumption and voyeuristic pleasure of his party guests. Ahasuerus commands his eunuchs to "bring Queen Vashti before the king, wearing the royal crown, in order to show the peoples and the officials her beauty" (1:11). It is possible that the king wants Vashti brought forth naked here (and thus utterly "opened"), wearing *only* the crown (White Crawford 2003: 330). Vashti refuses, and so faces violence through her deposition; subsequently, in an attempt to find her "replacement," the violence of abduction and rape is perpetrated against countless virgin girls, once again stressing the interchangeability and expendability of female bodies.

Moreover, as religious studies scholar Rhiannon Graybill has observed, the horror genre often identifies the opened female body as a means of negating and negotiating masculinity. Graybill points out that disturbance to and crises of hegemonic masculinity are intricately linked to the openness of the female body (2017: 64–65). Stated differently, torture, or the opening of the female body, becomes a way to speak about and around masculinity and masculine performance (2017: 52). For Graybill, openness and torture of female bodies thus reveal that masculinity is contested, problematized, and renegotiated in complicated – if not violent or frightening – ways (2017: 58). Masculinity is "unstable, rage-filled, impotent, acting with and acted upon by violence" (2017: 68). In the book of Esther, female bodies and masculinity are textual concerns that both set and drive the plot of the narrative. As I have discussed above, the bodies of women and girls in the Esther text are socially situated and regulated by colonizing men in their attempts to negotiate and mitigate their masculinity. As a result, multiple female bodies are subjected to outrageous and repeated violence throughout the opening two chapters.

A final feature of horror that is worth noting is its ability to evoke psychological responses within its audiences. As Kalmanofsky notes, "audience reactions are essential to the genre of horror as horror is identified by the reactions it elicits from the audience" (2008: 61). Audience reactions and responses to the biblical narrative are similar to what philosopher Noel Carroll describes as the "mirroring effect," wherein the terror, disgust, and fear expressed by *characters* within the horror text serve to provoke similar emotions in the consuming *audience* (1990: 18). Although the narrator does not directly comment, let alone dwell, on the fear or shock reactions of the characters in the text of Esther, many readers, when directed to them, can identify events in the text that give rise to fear, dread, or disgust.

In addition, persons who have been wounded by sexual, racialized, and other types of abuse tend to identify such abuse more easily in narrative than those who have not. Certainly, each time I read the text of Esther, the imagery of repeated sexual exploitation and the stereotyping of Africana girls and women and of other persons with subjugated identities terrify me. I am especially terrified when I consider the impact of this text in light of recent trends in trafficking. Another concern is the impact of horror on abused and trafficked girls and women who may be searching sacred scriptures for consolation and hope. Some may wonder if a function of this text was and, in contemporary contexts, still is to justify oppression, subjugation, and sexual violence against girls and women. A text of authority that reveals without criticism and outrage widespread practices of domination and oppression and one that could be used to justify the oppression of vulnerable humans, can be appalling to readers and interpreters alike.[15] After all, this is a sacred text that reflects legalization and facilitation of trafficking and exploitation of girls by the "government." The fact that the girls apparently never again leave the palace and remain the property of the king is horrendous. Even if the narrator excludes the responses and reactions of the virgin girls, the recorded details alone can trigger reactions of fear, helplessness, and hopelessness, especially among a collective of girls and women whose ancestors endured and who themselves continue to experience similarly gruesome conditions and encounters. The female collective in Esther consists of tormented girls and women who experience terror and pain. They are rendered helpless and immobilized by a seemingly unstoppable system embedded within patriarchal and colonial cultures. Girls and women across time and contexts who read the text of Esther may feel they can do nothing but anticipate inevitable woundedness and the terror that unavoidably ensues. Their pain seems inescapable.

By reading the book of Esther through the lens of horror, we are made more attuned to the social injustices and violations of human rights that occupy its pages. The first two chapters detail personal and collective experiences of injustice toward the female characters presented therein. Specifically, the book features unnumbered nameless Africana girls who contend with experiences of colonization, displacement, and sexual trafficking. They are vulnerable to oppression and sexual abuse for three long years before becoming the king's concubines, which undoubtedly exposes them to restriction, confinement, and further sexual abuse. Their agency, autonomy, and voices are suppressed, while male imperial representatives ensure their utter abandonment and isolation. Read as a horror text, the book of Esther invites us, the audience, to share the fear and terror of these trafficked girls. Moreover, the terror within the text becomes amplified, urging readers to recognize the deep injustices perpetrated against Africana females in the name of empire, patriarchy, and colonialism, and then to challenge these, both within the narrative itself and in other as well as our own contemporary contexts. Distressing as these stories are, they are a source of knowledge that describes and validates pain, terror, and injustices inflicted and inscribed on the bodies, psyches, and spirits of Africana women and girls in contexts of empire.

When we read the book of Esther as a horror story, it has the potential to connect experiences of trauma and subsequent violent acts. Horror and violence impact and influence people in diverse ways. And sometimes, persons who experience horrific violence internalize abuse as conduct to be imitated. In this way, violence can be a learned behavior. Other times, victims of violence engage in violence to survive. The Jews in the story world live through the experience of having a legal bounty placed on them and there is no way to revoke the law; they may be imagined as having internalized the violence that they and other sub-groups (e.g., the virgin girls) experienced. Living in the diaspora with limited access to resources, they may have used physical violence for survival and to resist the threats of the Persian Empire. In other words, the book of Esther presents horrifying situations that have the potential to induce fear, aggression, and other forms of emotional instability, among those impacted by violence and horror.

The Jews of the story world are afraid of the Persian colonizers. They are especially afraid of Haman, who plots their destruction, and of the king, who authorizes their annihilation. Evidence of this fear is depicted as Esther's deference to Persian law when she is encouraged to speak up on the Jews' behalf (Esther 4), Mordecai's and the other Jews' weeping, lamenting, and covering themselves in sackcloth and ashes (Esther 4), Esther's careful and strategic invitations to banquets (Esther 5, 7), Esther's rhetoric and desperate plea to the king regarding the plight of the Jews (Esther 7) and Esther's subsequent weeping and pleading at the feet of the king (Esther 8). These story elements illustrate how horrors induce fear responses in a vulnerable minority group. The response of aggressive and destructive violence proposed in Esther 8 and carried out in Esther 9 could be understood as a reaction to the violence they endured. Although the narrator does not explicitly state the Jews' reason for deploying murderous violence, we, as contemporary consumers of horror and violence, might interpret it as reactive to threats to life and livelihood.

Smaller and calculated acts of resistance by the Jews in the book of Esther suggest that the communities that produced this literature endeavored to critique the systems and structures that oppressed them also in ways other than through brutal violence. However, a literary artifact that envisions violence can be understood as an aggressive response. Attention to features of horror in biblical texts raises important questions about readers' responses, about whether violent/

horrific acts in sacred texts are used to legitimize current practices of abuse, and about the impacts of the depiction of violence and horror in sacred texts on individual and group identities and memories. I will go on to outline other trauma responses and consequences of traumatization commonly experienced by those targeted by sexual violence.

Other horrific implications of sexual trafficking

Next, I will outline some of the physical, emotional, psychological, and spiritual consequences to further illuminate the horror of sexual trafficking. Those who are trafficked often live and work in horrific conditions that involve isolation, deprivation, torture, and other forms of physical and psychosocial abuse. Many victims experience negative physical and health consequences including sexually transmitted infections, infertility, developmental challenges, teen and unwanted pregnancies, and unsafe abortions. Psychological effects include lowered self-esteem, depression, posttraumatic stress disorder (PTSD), anxiety, distress, eating disorders, substance abuse, nightmares, suicidal ideation and attempts, stress, dissociation, panic disorders, and engagement in other high-risk behaviors that render them yet more vulnerable to abuse (In Their Shoes"). Moreover, even long after abuse has occurred, such mundane things as receiving a hug, or trips to hair and nail shops, or to a department store to pick up clothes or perfume, can trigger negative emotional reactions, because these acts, too, may have played a part in the meticulously organized processes that subjected victims to prolonged and repeated traumatization.

The presence of trauma negatively impacts Africana girls and women in unhealthy and psychologically harmful ways and has done so for generations. Many Africana girls and women resort to silence because of trauma. Others are silenced by those who perpetuate trauma and/or through oral and written "histories" that distort or ignore the record of such trauma. Nevertheless, the physical, spiritual, psychological, and emotional scars speak, even if they are not always articulated in words. Trauma, shame, and history live in Africana females' bodies and memories. The language of many Africana females' bodies reflects what the field of epigenetics is beginning to uncover: namely, scientific proof that trauma is absorbed into human DNA. Children are not merely repeating learned behaviors they have observed, wounded generations respond to trauma in their descendants' bodies. There are, in fact, *genetic ramifications for intergenerational transmissions of trauma.*

Sociologists Bridget Goosby and Chelsea Heidbrink outline some genetic ramifications of intergenerational and collective traumatization. Conducting research that utilizes the bio-psychosocial model of racism, Goosby and Heidbrink argue that structural and interpersonal racial discrimination are key factors and salient mechanisms perpetuating health disparities of Africana peoples and their offspring. These health consequences are transmitted generationally through the body's biological memory of harmful experiences influenced by violent and otherwise dysfunctional physical and social environments. In other words, racially discriminatory harmful practices and the embodiment of inequality are transmitted through epigenetic mechanisms. Chronic pain and acute distress alter a mother's and her offspring's genetic expression, which often results in overactive physiological responses, including deterioration and increased vulnerability to disease (2013: 630–643).

Alongside this, religious and spiritual effects include: challenges to one's faith; the self-perception of being a sinner and irredeemable; conflation of pimp and other parties involved in trafficking, with God/religious leaders; failure to perceive the church as a safe place to talk about sex and sexuality, or to perceive religious leaders as protective; experiences of blame, shame, and unworthiness; and feeling no protection under biblical laws, or feeling targeted, maligned or relegated to the status of chattel by biblical or other religious laws. Such understandings are prevalent in some contemporary contexts.[16] The use of religious actors and factors by traffickers to manipulate and control those at risk of and subjected to sexual trafficking is also documented in research. The forced migration and trade of slaves enabled white colonizers to spread their ideologies to different locales, including through religion. Colonizers, with deliberation, demonized, denigrated, and eradicated indigenous and traditional religions that could have enabled enslaved Africans to cope with and resist exploitative practices. They substituted these religions with Christianity and justified their practices with selective teachings from sacred texts, advancing their agendas of trade and abuse.

Additionally, religious institutions, many of which still subscribe to purity codes and principles that fetishize female virginity, marriage, and marital faithfulness, are often extremely judgmental of girls and women who have been sexually exploited. Some ostracize and find fault with girls and women for being sex workers yet fail to critique the cultures that facilitate rape, sexual exploitation and sex work, or the actions of the perpetrators. Stigmatizing and silencing of survivors' experiences of abuse can contribute to mistrust or rejection of religious leaders and institutions. If abusees see no support, outrage, or other vocal support from authorities or institutions of faith, they can and do interpret such actions as indifference to or even complicity in abuse. Moreover, exploited girls and women often experience high occurrences of STDs and abortions. Again, both are strongly associated with shame and stigma and are weaponized particularly against marginalized and minoritized girls and women. Once more, religious and religio-political actors are often at the forefront of such attacks, judgments, and moral aspersions. Further, they weigh in on and legislate about abortion, even in cases of rape, other traumatic experiences, or maternal health, regularly pressuring or preventing pregnant women from making decisions about their own bodies, and wellbeing. These actions have some correspondence with those of the imperial agents in the book of Esther. Here, too, fear and anxiety around female agency and empowerment bring about gendered laws that function to control and oppress the female collective and female bodies.

Moreover, there are trends of traffickers appropriating and subverting religious language which lend themselves to instilling and demanding unquestioning obedience. Some survivors of trafficking note that the rhetoric of traffickers and abusers resembles that of the deity in sacred texts and of some religious leaders in contemporary contexts. For example, perpetrators of sexual abuse, both traffickers and pimps, position themselves as "gods" demanding worship and loyalty. Interestingly, when I have spoken to girls and women who have been abused, they reflect on this conflation noting that pimps often appropriate biblical rhetoric, using expressions such as, "I am your god," or "I am your protector," or "I provide your needs." Traffickers thereby apply and distort that which is normalized in spiritual and religious settings to advance their objectives. Such language also supports male dominance and control, and female subservience. It is indeed troubling to imagine spiritual and religious language and imagery causing or perpetuating harm but this is the testimony of some persons who survive trafficking. And when they go on to turn to religious and spiritual organizations for hope or support with processing and overcoming trauma, this can have retraumatizing potential. Spiritual practitioners must consider the impact of sacred texts, as well as the impact of the interpretations they disseminate, on individuals and on cultural groups that have experienced wide-scale sexualized abuse. The Bible includes many stories of sexualized violence against individuals and collectives, particularly of minoritized and marginalized girls and women of diverse ethnic groups. In reading these horrifying stories and engaging with interpretations that may justify or fail to acknowledge and resist sexualized abuse, the potential of vicarious traumatization, horror responses, and other negative implications for readers must be kept in view.

There are also economic and legal considerations. While traffickers stand to gain financially, those trafficked often remain entrapped in cycles of poverty. Trafficked persons are often lacking or are actively denied access to education and the acquisition of marketable skills. Regularly, they do not have information about even their most basic rights. Moreover, the trafficked experience wage theft, and, frequently, language and other cultural barriers, leading to obstructed and diminished opportunities for advancement, or even awareness of any available options. Many lack work permits, or even the paperwork or immigrant status to apply legally for work. This is strongly reminiscent of the Maafa, which also enabled traffickers to boost their economies by violently extracting peoples from their homes, depriving them of any dignity and rights, and exploiting them for free labor. During the Maafa, only the colonial masters, traffickers, and their collaborators profited from this highly lucrative economy, while those enslaved suffered profound material, economic, psychological, spiritual, physical, social, and other disastrous and traumatic consequences including sexual abuse. The brutal manifestations of capitalism in both colonial and up-to-the-present trafficking cultures produce horrific consequences for those that experience their exploitation and inequities. These are far from limited to the direct victims but have widespread repercussions, such as on economic destabilization, theft of land, destruction of ecosystems, and dismemberment of communities and, epigenetically, on subsequent generations. Moreover, not only are people, their energy, and potential, alongside land and natural resources consumed, but so is violence. The consumption of mass violence, in turn, impacts and infects both the consumed and the consumer – as we saw also played out in the final chapters of the book of Esther, where the Jews enact the type of violence that threatened their own existence. This shows that entrapment in cycles of impoverishment and violence has terrifying and ongoing repercussions.

The physical and spiritual injuries on human individuals and collectives result from histories of sexual enslavement and colonization, which are firmly entwined. These injuries have not only diminished individuals' senses of self and transformed Africana females' DNA but have also faded the collective's sense of self and exterminated many of the collective's cultural and spiritual traditions. If any further damage to Africana females' bodies, psyches, and souls is to be curtailed, responses must be comprehensive, holistic. And one tool of resistance in the arsenal must be polyvocal intersectional analysis of sacred texts and other historical documents. This is not only because of what such analysis brings to collective Africana memory but also because robust interdisciplinary assessment of the vast and cumulative impact of sexual trafficking and abuse against the Africana female collective is crucial and urgent.

Because the book of Esther is written from the perspective of the Jews, it serves as a record or testimony of the types of abuse they experienced at the hands of Persian colonizers, namely the threat of genocide. However, because of narrative silencing, the euphemisms embedded within the text, and the framing of the sexualized abuse by contemporary interpreters in terms of beauty pageantry, many readers fail to perceive that Vashti and the virgin girls are subjected to sexualized abuse. Even though sexualized abuse is explicitly referred to, readers never gain access to the voices, insights, perspectives, or testimonies of the virgin girls who are fleetingly mentioned in this "Jewish" text. Thus, it is important for me to foreground their experiences and to challenge the silence, invisibility, and harm perpetuated against them. Moreover, the lawmakers in the story world, who are among the colonizers, create laws grounded in stereotypes and general assumptions about how certain groups will behave. For example, when Vashti is deposed for refusing to be paraded before the drunken king and his inebriated officials and ministers, a law is created and used as a tool to assert and reassert male control and dominance over the female collective. The judicial sentencing, that "every man be master in his own household," is made in retaliation to Vashti's refusal and to send a warning to other women who *might be inspired* by her resistance (1:17–18). Another example of stereotyping is Haman's statement in 3:8 (aforementioned) where he describes the Jews as "a certain people" with "different" laws, who defy the king's laws and regarding whom it is acceptable to be intolerant. Following this reductive stereotyping, it becomes an easy matter for Haman to petition the king to issue a decree for the Jews' destruction (3:9), which is granted (3:10). That the king and his officials can make and enforce laws based on speculation and stereotyping, brings to mind issues of accountability, connected to yet another horror related to sexual trafficking: the low reporting of abuse. To whom could either the scattered Jews of the Persian Empire, or the trafficked virgin girls report their abuse? How could they hold the king accountable for his actions when they were part of and victim to the colonial enterprise?

In contemporary contexts, fear of consequences of reporting abuse and underreporting, help to enable the horrors of sexual trafficking.

Although reported rates of sexual violence are high and (in some parts of the world) growing, there are believed to be much higher rates of unreported incidences, because women and girls are often reluctant to approach police and other officials. This reluctance can be attributed partly to victims' suspicion and fear of officialdom, and partly to the social and cultural attitudes that devalue women's and girls' rights before the law, as is evidenced, for instance, by very low conviction rates for sexual offenses. In many instances, victims are deterred from coming forward by local, state, or governments' neglect and refusal to protect them, or even to investigate their claims, or hold perpetrators responsible.[17] Moreover, those abused are often silenced or their character maligned by media outlets. These are issues being raised and challenged by the #SayHerName movement.

Other reasons for underreporting include: fear of retaliation, judgment by others, or self-blame. Because perpetrators use their social and cultural status to assert power over less privileged persons, the vulnerable can feel coerced to comply and/or may have anxieties about what may happen if they do not comply, try to escape, or report perpetrators. Others may engage in self-blaming attitudes in response to their inability to avoid and/or escape manipulative situations. Moreover, psychological manipulation may lead to the inability of the vulnerable to identify a trafficker as an abuser or may prevent the exploited from reporting the abuse. This may further result in the abusee blaming herself for being in a situation beyond their control and taking on responsibility for their abuse, which may be perceived as a means for the abused to take back a sense of control. Additionally, self-blame can be exacerbated by feelings of hopelessness and resignation, which may result from traffickers' claims that no one cares about the abusee's plight and feelings of powerlessness, or communities' failure to take a stance against trafficking ("In Their Shoes," Polaris 2021). The above-outlined experiences not only present challenges to sex trafficking research but also prevent abusees and survivors from obtaining justice.

Sociologist and anthropologist Karen G. Weiss notes that negative emotions experienced by rape victims frequently include shame, which, in turn, significantly shapes self-value and self-esteem (2010: 286). Shame, while a universal experience with many causes, commonly affects victims of sexual trafficking. Oftentimes, abuse is masked by pervasive secrecy and shame, which lead on to stigmatization of rape disclosure. For example, perpetrators might shame the vulnerable with their poverty, lack of education or a job, or by condemning physical features. Other times, those abused might experience shame because of their perception of who they are or have become through trafficking. Many survivors report feelings of humiliation, disgrace, dehumanization, and shame not only due to exploitation but also because of rejection by and disdainful responses from family and community members (Nathanson 1987: 3). These rejections and responses may derive from judgments based on sexual activity itself, or from other things associated with sex work and trafficking, such as substance abuse, perceived promiscuity or immorality, pregnancy, abortion, miscarriage, or losing children to child welfare systems. Any of these traumatic and stigmatizing emotional experiences can negatively and profoundly affect victims for sustained periods of time – and shaming intensifies these experiences.

Disclosing exploitation inevitably increases a victim's visibility, possibly exposing them to ridicule, blame, and other negative responses already noted above. Disclosure can also result in revisiting a painful experience, as well as the increased risks of being exposed, identified, vilified, or even criminalized (Anderson and Doherty 2008: 3). Sometimes victims who disclose are publicly disparaged or attacked, which intensifies shame and anxiety, inferiority, and defeat (Tomkins 1987: 143). Psychologist Gershen Kaufman notes that the effect of shame is a heightened awareness of the self, which often results in persons feeling exposed, as though examined under a microscope (2004: 22). Often, visibility, or hypervisibility, involves, alongside self-scrutiny, also additional external scrutiny, because the case, or situation of sexual exploitation marks the victim out as "different," or "newsworthy." This can be compounded by factors such as race, class, gender, or physical abilities, as Crenshaw has claimed because all of these can exacerbate the perception of a victim as "other." Kaufman adds that people who belong to minoritized cultural and racial groups, and who feel outcast or inferior because of it, are particularly prone to experiencing such social pressures as shame, as well as to magnified feelings of powerlessness (2004: 299). Disclosure of abuse, therefore, presents dilemmas, because, on the one hand, invisibility and silence enable sexual trafficking to thrive, yet, on the other, visibility and vocality regarding abuse can produce negative consequences, especially for persons already marginalized and minoritized, such as Africana girls and women.

Another challenge to researching child sex trafficking, and to prosecuting traffickers is that often the abuse and exploitation of children is a cultural norm, sanctioned by attitudes that suggest that men have a right to engage in sex with underage girls, or that girls are responsible for inciting sexual attention and assault by the way they behave or dress. Moreover, many child victims are accused of promiscuity, running away, or criminalized for truancy or sex work, while perpetrators experience low rates of arrest and prosecution. Far too many minors are vulnerable to prosecution because of the failure of society and legal entities to recognize them as survivors of abuse. This enables perpetrators to resume their heinous crimes. Related to this point and analogous to what we see in the book of Esther, in many contemporary contexts, males dominate courtroom spaces and hold positions of power in other legal/criminal justice structures, e.g., as judges, lawyers, jurors, and court officers. Therefore, many female victims perceive that justice will be compromised, or jeopardized, because these agents, whose duty it is to serve and protect, lack, or are believed to lack empathy, or to have ethical convictions. This is unfortunate because police and court officials play a major role in the fate and recovery of victims post traumatization. Since men continue to dominate legal systems, laws continue to be made that undermine justice for female victims of sexual trafficking. For example, in a number of more recent legal cases in the United States, Africana girls who are *victims* of sexual trafficking have been charged for killing their abusers and traffickers. Cyntoia Brown, Chrystal Kizer, and Alexis Martin are three women, all exploited in their childhood, whose experiences testify to the ongoing trafficking of African diasporic girls and women. Their arrests, trials, and treatment expose the failures of the justice system afforded to vulnerable minoritized women. Similar to Vashti's fate when she exercised resistance, we see that their acts of speaking out and protecting themselves led to each of these women being criminalized and "put away." This served to make them yet more marginalized and to render them silenced and invisible.

Not only are the acts of sexual violence horrific, but the subsequent silent suffering, blame, shame, scrutiny, neglect, notorious underreporting, few to no implications for perpetrators and facilitators, criminalization of the abused, invisibility, hypervisibility, the failure of loved ones and legal entities to protect the abused, helplessness of family members, and increased marginalization, all contribute to the above outlined psychological responses, evoked by horror, that are far too often experienced by trafficked Africana girls and women. Therefore, challenges to researching trafficking not only perpetuate silence of the abuse but also mute the stories and histories, and endeavor to muffle the collective memories of numerous collectives experiencing sexualized violence. These practices exacerbate the trauma in ways that increase the horror. Not knowing the full extent of, the parties involved in, or the mechanisms of trafficking continues to mask the full scope and impact of the abuse and traumatization on Africana girls' and women's bodies, psyches, identities, memories, both on the African continent and throughout the diaspora. None of these issues are humorous. They are unequivocally horrific. This applies to trafficking and other physical and sexual abuse, to the staggering statistics, and to the multiple ways that society fails to respond to crimes and assailants. Alongside a lack of focus and energy invested in transforming societies and cultures toward the prevention and reduction of harm enacted against Africana girls and women these are, I repeat, unequivocally horrific.

Esther, when reading as horror, allows readers and interpreters to identify and foreground depictions of horrifying injustice. From there, we can supplement textual analysis with identification and critiques of sexually violent atrocities across other contexts. Horror creates a hyperawareness of sexualized violence, including that enacted against Africana females, and can finally foster a generation of biblical engagers who will become frightened by the ways that ethnicity, class, gender, and other indicators of identity are weaponized against those rendered marginal in ancient and present societies. Horror can galvanize those same frightened readers to act on behalf of those harmed and oppressed. Horror has the potential to help readers not only to identify evil, ghostly, and monstrous spirits and human beings but also to identify, call out, and critique evil ideologies, practices, and embodiments of power in both the biblical text and in contemporary contexts.

In this chapter, I have illustrated that in general, patriarchs and colonizers use stereotypes and make ideological claims about the disenfranchised to justify their abuse. Specifically, in the book of Esther, the male collective offered stereotypes about the Jews and about the female collective to justify creating biased laws that would invoke horror, terror, shock, and suffering. Similarly, in the US colonial context, colonizers used stereotypes about Africana female sexuality to justify sexual violence and enslavement. This positioned Africana girls and women as vulnerable to rape and led to trafficking and torture during the Maafa and into the twenty-first century. These racialized gender stereotypes are but one example of the forms of intersectional oppression Africana girls and women endure, especially in colonized and postcolonial contexts.

I probed some of the textual euphemisms embedded within the book of Esther along with silences and cover-ups by interpreters that often obscure the depiction of sexual trafficking. These cover-ups further perpetuate silence and secrecy among Africana females regarding their abuse. Finally, I argue that readers and interpreters should read the book of Esther through the lens of horror as it enables readers to identify and amplify the sexualized violence enacted against the female collective in the book of Esther and, to acknowledge both individual and collective traumatization across contexts. The application of horror further enables readers to consider the impact of abuse on Africana females' bodies, psyches, and identities. In the final chapter, I will summarize my interpretative findings and offer some implications for my distinctive, socially located reading of the book of Esther.

Notes

1 See Carolyn West, "Mammy, Sapphire, and Jezebel: Historical Images of Black Women and Their Implications for Psychotherapy," in *Psychotherapy: Theory, Research, Practice and Training* Vol. 32, no. 3 (1995): 458–466; Melissa Harris-Perry, *Sister Citizen: Shame, Stereotypes and Black Women in America* (New Haven; London: Yale University Press, 2011); Traci C. West, *Wounds of the Spirit: Black Women, Violence and Resistance Ethics* (New York: NYU Press, 1999); Roxanne Donovan and Michelle Williams, "Living at the Intersection: The Effects of Racism and Sexism on Black Rape Survivors," in *Women & Therapy* Vol. 25, no. 3–4 (2002): 95–105; Ella L. Bell, "Myths Stereotypes, and Realities of Black Women: A Personal Reflection," in *The Journal of Applied Behavioral Science* Vol. 28, no. 3 (1992): 363–376.
2 It is also ironic that the Jews are commanded to blot out the memory of the Amalekites, yet the Amalekites are remembered each time the story is told and each year when Purim is celebrated.
3 See Edward Said, *Orientalism: Western Concepts of the Orient* (New York: Pantheon, 1978).
4 In a similar way, the lavish description of banquets and rich furnishings in the early chapters of Esther become metaphorically linked in the imagination with the minoritized girls from all over the empire. Here too "exotic virgin girls" are cast in a background of abundance to stimulate sexual fantasy.
5 See Mimi Sheller, "Natural Hedonism: The Invention of Caribbean Islands as Tropical Playgrounds," in *Tourism in the Caribbean: Trends, Development, Prospects*, edited by David Duval (London and New York: Routledge, 2004), 23–28.
6 Vincent Wimbush points out that biblical scholarship has a legacy of Western cultural domestication and containment, which he identifies as the "Europeanization of the Bible that the separation from the past from the present has fostered and made evident." In other words, there is a "tendency to think that the Bible was written for, speaks to and can be appropriately and authoritatively interpreted only by Europeans, that the ancient cultural streams that it represents flow directly into European settings." This propensity ultimately leads to what he deems "fetishization of a certain class-specific cultural text interpretative practice." Wimbush posits that when we foreground African Americans in the academic study of the Bible, and I would broaden this to include African diasporic

106 *Social and cultural attitudes*

subjects outside of America as well, we have a radically different orientation in the discourse. This type of foregrounding "forces readers to come to terms with and see the full complexity of American history and the full range and complexity of human emotions, foibles, risings, and fallings through the experiences of African Americans." See, Vincent Wimbush, "Interrupting the Spin: What Might Happen If African Americans Were to Become the Starting Point for the Academic Study of the Bible," in *Union Seminary Quarterly Review* Vol. 52 (1998): 61–76.
7 For more on Esther as social and political satire, see Kenneth Craig Jr., *Reading Esther: A Case for Literary Carnivalesque* (Louisville: Westminster John Knox Press, 1995).
8 According to Akoto, Vashti's actions show women's power at work in the empire and court. Such is clearly conducive to inciting male anxiety. Akoto, 270.
9 See "Nigerian Chibok Abductions: What We Know," BBC, May 8, 2017. Accessed March 15, 2021, https://www.bbc.com/news/world-africa-32299943.
10 In addition, Nigerian Correspondent Mayeni Jones notes that many abductions took place before the 2014 abduction, but they did not involve girls and received little publicity. She writes that the 2014 raid gained global traction because of the social medial campaign #BringBackOurGirls. Social media campaigns can and do transform the silence and invisibility that enables this type of maltreatment to thrive and applies pressure on authorities to combat and prosecute perpetrators of abuse. See "Nigeria's Zamfara School Abduction: More than 300 Nigerian Girls Missing," *BBC*, February 26, 2021. Accessed March 16, 2021, https://www.bbc.com/news/world-africa-56188727.
11 See Kevin M. McGeough, "The Roles of Violence in Recent Biblical Cinema: The Passion, Noah, and Exodus: God and Kings," in *Journal of Religion and Film* Vol. 20, no. 2 (2016): 1–53.
12 For example, see Rhiannon Graybill, *Are We Not Men? Unstable Masculinity in the Hebrew Bible* (New York: Oxford University Press, 2017); Amy Kalmanofsky, "Israel's Baby: The Horror of Childbirth in the Biblical Prophets," in *Biblical Interpretation* Vol. 16 (2008): 60–82; and Steve Wiggins, *Holy Horror: The Bible and Fear in Movies* (Jefferson, NC: McFarland & Company, 2018).
13 Tina Pippin, *Apocalyptic Bodies: The Biblical End of the World in Text and Image* (London: Routledge, 2002), 80, citing Freud, 1958, 219.
14 For examples of the abjection of virgin female bodies in horror texts and films, see Angela Carter's short story "Bluebird" in *The Bloody Chamber* (1979), *Texas Chainsaw Massacre* (1974), *Black Christmas* (1974, 2006), and *Halloween* (1978, 2007). Also see *Very Young Girls* (2007), a documentary following two trafficked teenage African American girls in New York, who are treated by law enforcement as adult criminals.
15 For examples and commentary on how the Bible has been used to support and justify enslavement and other violently oppressive behaviors, see: Emerson B. Powery and Rodney S Sadler, *The Genesis of Liberation: Biblical Interpretation in Antebellum Narratives of the Enslaved* (Louisville: Westminster John Knox, 2016); Noel Rae, *The Great Stain: Witnessing American Slavery* (New York: Overlook Press, 2018); and Stephen Hayes, *Noah's Curse: The Biblical Justification of American Slavery* (Oxford: Oxford University Press, 2007).

16 Bryant-Davis et al. note that some religious beliefs are used to blame and justify the sexual violation of females, or to shame them for the effects of assault. Further, religious leaders have sometimes used religious texts to objectify and demonize sexualized females. See Thema Bryant-Davis, Heewoon Chung, and Shaquita Tillman, "From the Margins to the Center: Ethnic Minority Women and the Mental Health Effects of Sexual Assault," in *Trauma, Violence & Abuse* Vol. 10, no. 4 (2009): 348.

17 See Global Law Enforcements data on page 43 of the 2020 Trafficking in Persons report, US Department of State, *Trafficking in Persons Report 20th Edition* (Washington, DC: US Department of State Publications, 2020), accessed July 14, 2021, https://www.state.gov/wp-content/uploads/2020/06/2020-TIP-Report-Complete-062420-FINAL.pdf. These statistics are estimates derived from reports by foreign governments and other sources and include several types of trafficking, not merely sex trafficking offenses. The actual numbers are unknown due to several factors including but not limited to the hidden and underground nature of trafficking, lack of reporting, the lack of uniformity in reporting, no legislation on trafficking, and/or laws that criminalize only certain aspects of trafficking. According to this 2020 report, globally, in 2019, there were nearly 11,841 persecutions and 9,548 convictions. Yet, the US Secretary of State acknowledges that at least 25 million people were trafficked. This shows a tremendous gap in occurrences of trafficking and prosecutions/convictions. The United Nations Office of Drugs and Crimes Global Report on Trafficking In Persons 2020 also reflects that underreporting is an issue that prevents us from ascertaining the magnitude of the scope, scale, and impact of trafficking. According to the report, data collected from 163 countries showed that only about 15,800 total cases of trafficking (in all forms) were either investigated or prosecuted (https://www.unodc.org/unodc/data-and-analysis/glotip.html). See: United Nations Office on Drugs and Crimes, *Global Report on Trafficking in Persons 2020* (New York: United Nations Publications, January 2021), accessed July 14, 2021, https://www.unodc.org/documents/data-and-analysis/tip/2021/GLOTiP_2020_15jan_web.pdf

Works Cited

Anderson, Irina, and Kathy Doherty. *Accounting for Rape: Psychology, Feminism, and Discourse Analysis in the Study of Sexual Violence.* New York: Routledge, 2008.

Bailey, Randall C. "That's Why They Didn't Call the Book Hadassah!": The Interse(ct)/(x)ionality of Race/Ethnicity, Gender, and Sexuality in the Book of Esther." In *They Were All Together in One Place? Toward Minority Biblical Criticism.* Randall Bailey, Tat-Siong Benny Liew, and Fernando Segovia, eds. Atlanta: Society of Biblical Literature, 2009: 227–250.

Bravo, Karen E. "Black Female 'Things' in International Law: A Meditation on Saartjie Baartman and Truganini." *Black Women and International Law: New Theory, Old Praxis.* Cambridge: Cambridge University Press, Robert H. McKinney School of Law, Legal Studies Research Paper No 12–25, 2012: 1–38.

Bryant-Davis, Thema and Pratyusha Tummala-Narra. "Cultural Oppression and Human Trafficking: Exploring the Role of Racism and Ethnic Bias." *Women & Therapy* 40, Nos. 1–2 (2017): 152–169.

Bryant-Davis, Thema, Heewoon Chung, and Shaquita Tillman. "From the Margins to the Center: Ethnic Minority Women and the Mental Health Effects of Sexual Assault." *Trauma, Violence, & Abuse* 10, no. 4 (2009): 330–357.

Butler, Cheryl N. "A Critical Race Feminist Perspective on Prostitution & Sex Trafficking in America." *Yale JL & Feminism* 27 (2015a): 95–139.

———. "Racial Roots of Human Trafficking." *UCLA Law Review* 62, (2015b): 1464–1514.

Carroll, Noel. *The Philosophy of Horror or Paradoxes of the Heart.* New York: Routledge, 1990.

Chong, Natividad G. "Human Trafficking and Sex Industry: Does Ethnicity and Race Matter?" *Journal of Intercultural Studies* 35, no. 2 (2014): 196–213.

Christensen, Carole. "Issues in Sex Therapy with Ethnic and Racial Minority Women." *Women & Therapy* 7, Nos. 2–3 (1988): 187–205.

Crenshaw, Kimberlé. "Demarginalizing the Intersection of Race and Sex: A Black Feminist Critique of Antidiscrimination Doctrine, Feminist Theory and Antiracist Politics." *University of Chicago Legal Forum* 140 (1989): 139–167.

Duran, Nicole. "Who Wants to Marry a Persian King? Gender Games and Wars and the Book of Esther." In *Pregnant Passion: Gender, Sex, and Violence in the Bible.* Cheryl A. Kirk-Duggan, ed. Leiden: Brill, 2004: 71–84.

Fox, Michael V. *Character and Ideology in the Book of Esther.* Second Edition. Grand Rapids: William B. Eerdmans Publishing Company, 1991.

Goosby, Bridget and Chelsea Heidbrink. "Transgenerational Consequences of Racial Discrimination for African American Health." *Social Compass* 7, no. 8 (August 2013): 630–643.

Graybill, Rhiannon. *Are We Not Men? Unstable Masculinity in the Hebrew Bible.* New York: Oxford University Press, 2017.

Hill Collins, Patricia. *Black Feminist Thought: Knowledge, Consciousness and the Politics of Empowerment.* New York: Routledge, 2000.

"Horror," in *Oxford English Dictionary Online.* September 2021. Oxford University Press. Accessed Septerber 27, 2021 https://www-oed-com.exproxy.princeton.edu/view/Entry?88577?result=1$rskey=DWMm3L&

Jones, Bruce. "Two Misconceptions about the Book of Esther." In *Studies in the Book of Esther*, Carey Moore, ed. New York: Ktav Publishing House, 1982: 171–181.

Kalmanofsky, Amy. "Israel's Baby: The Horror of Childbirth in the Biblical Prophets." *Biblical Interpretation* 16 (2008): 60–82.

Kaufman, Gershen. *The Psychology of Shame: Theory and Treatment of Shame-Based Syndromes.* Second Edition. New York: Springer Publishing Company, 2004.

Morrison, Toni. *The Pieces I Am Documentary*, directed by Timothy Greenfield-Sanders. New York: Magnolia Pictures, 2019.

Nadar, Sarojini. "'Texts of Terror' – The Conspiracy of Rape in the Bible, Church and Society: The Case of Esther 2: 1–18." In *African Women, Religion, and Health: Essays in Honor of Mercy Amba Ewudziw.* Isabel Apawo Phiri and Sarojini Nadar, eds. Eugene: Wipf and Stock, 2006: 77–95.

Nathanson, Donald. "A Timetable for Shame." In *The Many Faces of Shame.* Donald Nathanson, ed. New York: The Guilford Press, 1987: 1–62.

O'Connor, Kathleen M. "Humor, Turnabouts and Survival in the Book of Esther." In *Are We Amused: Humour About Women in the Biblical World.* Athalya Brenner, ed. London: T&T Clark International, 2003: 52–64.

Pippin, Tina. *Apocalyptic Bodies: The Biblical End of the World in Text and Image.* London: Routledge, 2002.

Said, Edward *Orientalism: Western Concepts of the Orient.* New York: Pantheon, 1978.

Sheller, Mimi. "Natural Hedonism: The Invention of Caribbean Islands as Tropical Playgrounds." In *Tourism in the Caribbean: Trends, Development, Prospects.* David Duval, ed. London and New York: Routledge, 2004: 23–28.

Stargel, Linda. *The Construction of Exodus Identity in Ancient Israel: A Social Identity Approach.* Eugene: Pickwick Publications, 2018.

Tillman, Shaquita, Thema Bryant-Davis, Kimberly Smith and Allison Marks. "Shattering the Silence: Exploring Barriers to Disclosure of African American Assault Survivors." *Trauma, Violence & Abuse* 11, no. 2 (April 2010): 59–70.

Tomkins, Silvan A. "Shame." In *The Many Faces of Shame.* Donald Nathanson, ed. New York: The Guilford Press, 1987: 133–161.

"In Their Shoes: Understanding Victims' Mindsets and Common Barriers to Victim Identification," Polaris. Accessed March 16, 2021, https://humantraffickinghotline.org/sites/default/files/Understanding%20Victim%20Mindsets.pdf

Weiss, Karen G. "Too Ashamed to Report: Deconstructing the Shame of Sexual Victimization." *Feminist Criminology* 5, no. 3 (2010): 286–310.

West, Carolyn. "Mammy, Sapphire and Jezebel: Historical Images of Black Women and their Implications for Psychotherapy." *Psychotherapy* 32, no. 3 (Fall 1995): 458–466.

West, Traci C. "A Moral Epistemology of Gender Violence." In *Ethics That Matters: African, Caribbean and African American Sources.* Marcia Y. Riggs and James Samuel Logan, eds. Minneapolis: Fortress Press, 2012: 171–184.

———. *Solidarity and Defiant Spirituality: Africana Lessons on Religion, Racism, and Engendering Gender Violence.* New York: New York University Press, 2019.

———. *Wounds of the Spirit: Black Women, Violence and Resistance Ethics.* New York: NYU Press, 1999.

White Crawford, Sidnie Ann. "Esther and Judith: Contrasts in Character." In *The Book of Esther in Modern Research.* Sidnie White Crawford and Leonard Greenspoon, eds. New York: T & T Clark International, 2003: 61–76.

4 "For Such a Time as This?"

Conclusions and Implications of Intersectional Polyvocal Africana Biblical Interpretation

This book offers an activist exploration of the intersections between sexual trafficking, gender, ethnicity, and class, both in the book of Esther and in the experiences and histories of diasporized Africana girls and women. Many biblical scholars note the centrality of gender in the characterizations of Vashti, Esther, and (though considerably less often) the female virgins and the eunuchs in this biblical book. However, less attention has been given to the roles of ethnicity, colonization, and minoritization in contributing to exposure to sexual exploitation and abuse. Also neglected are female experiences and perspectives of such exploitation. I argue that applying theories of intersectionality and polyvocality opens up the text, exposing additional imbedded and oppressive ideologies. These highlight that the Africana girls in the book of Esther are oppressed not solely on the basis of their gender but at the convergence of their gendered, ethnic, and classed identities.

Therefore, I bring together Africana, postcolonial, and trauma theory elements toward engaging in an intersectional, polyvocal reading of the book of Esther. Specifically, I employ Africana biblical criticism and black feminist, womanist, and postcolonial critical methodologies to position the particularities of Africana life, history, and culture at the center of the interpretative process. I investigate and describe sexual trafficking in cultural, historical, and literary contexts to demonstrate that this scourge disproportionately impacts minority and minoritized female collectives in multiple contexts. I consider how patriarchs, colonizers, and traffickers create and utilize trade and trafficking routes to sustain exploitative systems and institutions of sexual violence that hurt and fragment Africana girls, women, and their collective memories and identities, not only directly but also onwards through subsequent generations.

I show how some scholars interpreting the book of Esther have addressed life under imperial domination, and how others have

DOI: 10.4324/9781003168911-5

downplayed or disregarded diasporized vulnerability. I give particular attention to beauty, pageantry, humor, secrecy and hiding, euphemisms, and stereotypes, as well as their roles in sexual trafficking enterprises. Examining this constellation of themes together paints a vivid picture of conditions that produce and sustain sexual trafficking – in antiquity, during the Maafa, and in contemporary settings. In addition, it becomes clear that the diverse mechanisms of sexual trafficking are situated in broader contexts of colonialism and capitalism, and characterized by kyriarchy, patriarchy, gender hierarchies, political conflicts, abuses of power, domination, and brutal physical and sexual violence, as well as by survival in these hostile contexts.

The opening chapter of Esther introduces problematic gendered relationships between male and female characters. Vashti is deposed for resisting the king's demand to display herself before his drunken (male) party guests (Est. 1:10–12). This gendered conflict is one where the personal becomes intertwined with the political. Hence, the conflict shifts from being a dispute between a husband and wife (Ahasuerus and Vashti), to Vashti's sexualized exploitation being reframed as an offense against the king, his officials, and all the men that live in the king's provinces (1:16). As a result of one woman's (reasonable) refusal to be objectified, collective action is taken to prevent *all women* from imitating Vashti. A law is written, that "every man be master in his own household" (1:22), and it is explicitly stated that this law is written, "so that it may not be repealed" (1:19), thus sealing it into imperial legal codes in perpetuity.

But by focusing exclusively or even primarily on Vashti's and Esther's experiences of exploitation, traditional interpretations demonstrate an incomplete assessment of the geopolitical range and scope of sexual exploitation in the story. Such interpretations may reflect how the class and social status (i.e., the relative and conditional privilege) of Vashti and Esther cause interpreters to privilege the experiences of these two women over those of the many other girls and women alluded to in the text. But polyvocal intersectionality amplifies the voices and experiences of the many girls captured and brought to the harem and makes them an important part of the collective trauma enacted by the imperial policy.

When the treatment of the virgin girls depicted in the second chapter is assessed alongside the treatment of Vashti, it becomes clear that gender and ethnicity intersect and play a major role in othering foreign, minoritized females. Othered, these girls are rendered exploitable and consequently trafficked. Accordingly, the king's dismissal of Vashti is only a first step in a more elaborate process of imperially sanctioned patriarchy that also feeds sexual trafficking. By this process, the seeking out of girls is legitimated, as is their transport, custody, subjection to a year-long beautification process, and sexual abuse and exploitation by the king (2:1–9). The Persian king and his imperial team target African and other virgin girls for sexual trafficking. In its deployment of this political strategy, the text depicts Africana girls and women as expendable, commodifiable, and rapable. Such intentional displacement, colonization, and sexual exploitation of Africana girls and women are not, however, restricted to the pages of this biblical text, but have been practiced throughout much of history, leading to collective cultural trauma.

By foregrounding and prioritizing an intersectional, polyvocal, Africana hermeneutics in my reading of Esther 1–2, it becomes clear that many of the virgin girls come from geographical locales, including Ethiopia and India, that, in the present day, are predominantly inhabited by black and brown girls. Analogously, black and brown girls and women are disproportionately vulnerable to and targeted by sexual traffickers in contemporary contexts. This observation might help readers to understand why Africa was at the center of and foundational for the Maafa. Colonial forces constructed and promoted ideologies that "foreign" bodies, especially those of African descent, are inferior and not fully human; one consequence of this is that the crime of rape does not apply to Africana girls and women and that they do not need or deserve protection because they do not feel oppressed and are incapable of consent. My reading reveals not only the ethnically-charged hierarchical relationships and abuses of power in colonial and sexual trafficking institutions, but the propensity of colonizers of the "majority" or "powerful" ethnic group to target, exploit, and justify violently sexualized abuse of minoritized groups and bodies. I argue that these experiences of racist and gender-based violence in the form of sexual trafficking effected collective trauma that distills physical, sexual, and emotional experiences of sexual abuse and exploitation in this ancient context. Moreover, my interpretation emphasizes the traumatic and horrific experiences of the female collective which reflect profound and ingrained feelings of devastation, horror, and futility.

The depiction of sexual trafficking in the book of Esther has parallels with the cultural memories, histories, and pain of Africana girls and women across time and space, from the Persian empire to subsequent slave trade routes, and beyond, to the present. My reading of the text illuminates that Africana female bodies have been and continue to be colonized and sexualized, exploited for profit and pleasure, which has adverse physical, mental, sexual, and socio-cultural consequences.

Rendered sexual slaves, and perceived as less than human, Africana girls and women during the slave trade had no control over their lives, bodies, or sexual expression. Saartjie Baartman's story is another example of Africana collective trauma. Though she was born in South Africa, Baartman's body was transported, carnivalized, and put on display as an attraction in nineteenth-century Europe. Even after her death, her sexual organs and other body parts remained on display until as recently as 1974. I mentioned also Sally, an Africana girl enslaved by Thomas Thistlewood. Forced to migrate to Jamaica, Sally was raped by Thistlewood over 30 times, as recounted in his own chilling words. These are two of innumerable stories told and untold, which illustrate that sexual trafficking and sexual enslavement of girls and women were core experiences that have been and continue to be formative for identities of Africana females. Furthermore, these experiences were justified by racial stereotypes, such as the Jezebel myth, the Mammy figure, and the Sapphire trope, as well as by endemic social and cultural attitudes that encourage bias and normalize sexualized violence.

I apply collective memory theories to illuminate that such instances of sexual trafficking as the occurrences portrayed in the book of Esther and the countless incidents that took place during the transatlantic slave trade, inform Africana girls' and women's understandings of their individual and group selves, and enable them to reconstruct a past based on common identity. Experiences of sexual exploitation through trafficking are crystallized into the collective consciousness and memories of Africana females living on the continent and in the African diaspora. Their bodies store experiences of rape, enslavement, and forced impregnation and comprise histories that inform and impact the social, physical, economic, and psychological health of the collective. As such, they are tools of solidarity that provide a link to the past, present, and future. Moreover, they enable the group to reflect on identity and to articulate and collectively challenge ideologies, stereotypes, and actions applied to justify oppression and violence against them.

There is one more dimension to my polyvocal and intersectional interpretative spin: because the narrative is one that describes gendered violence, exploitation, and terror, I suggest the book of Esther should be considered as belonging to the genre of biblical horror. By reading the book of Esther as horror, we are made more emotionally attuned to the dreadfulness of the social injustices and violations of human rights in ancient and contemporary contexts. Reading Esther through the lens of the horror genre can highlight the intense trauma that underlies the book. This can encourage readers to engage empathetically with the injuries of both individuals and collectives that have too often historically been ignored and suppressed in both sacred and cultural narratives. And, in turn, emotional engagement can motivate us to confront actively and compassionately the horror and injustices perpetrated by sexual trafficking.

Attention to both the processes and parties involved in trafficking exposes the violent and horrific machinations of this text. Although the book of Esther is often read as comedy, or as a celebration of a beautiful and clever heroine who ascends to the Persian throne as queen – this does not tell the whole story, because it obscures, suppresses, and tacitly condones large-scale abuse. While this abuse is mostly mentioned succinctly, it is nevertheless substantial and includes the sexualized threat to Vashti, the sexual trafficking of many virgin girls, the attempt at genocide, and the actualization of mass murder at the book's close. Even more alarming, *all* these acts of threatened and actualized violence and oppression are legalized through imperial commands and edicts. Law-making thus becomes a means that drives the violent plot of the narrative, commencing with the sexual exploitation of females in the first two chapters and culminating with the effusively violent murder of Haman, his ten sons, and the enemies of the Jews.

Combining intersectionality, polyvocality, and attention to horror enables readers and interpreters to recognize multiple forms of one-off and of structural violence and to see the associations between the two. These frameworks open the text up in different and meaningful ways that draw attention to social and cultural injustices arising in societies marked by kyriarchy, colonialism, and patriarchy. The two contexts identified and assessed most closely in this book specifically illustrate that power, status, and wealth are achieved and accumulated by physically and sexually exploiting and oppressing Africana female bodies. Colonizers use laws to their advantage to accomplish their political goals of dominance and global status. They confiscate bodies, lands, and other material resources in violent ways to achieve these ends. Silence and erasure only stabilize such exploitative systems. When readers can recognize and understand intersectional oppressions, they develop empathy for those harmed and might become inspired to use their own agency, privilege, and power to transform victimizing systems and structures.

As a person committed to justice, I know that it is necessary that we, as contemporary recipients of this ancient text, identify, assess, and critique the violence that has many times been ignored, and even celebrated by individuals and groups. This is particularly urgent because this ancient text is revered and canonized and as such, continues to be made relevant and to be consulted for guidance up to the present. We must acknowledge the role that religions and sacred stories play in creating and maintaining hierarchies of power, as well as their impact on the psyches and identities of readers. Additionally, those who claim a Jewish or Christian identity must wrestle with the toxic content of biblical texts, be attentive to the injustices detailed within and to theologies that have been applied in contemporary contexts to maintain gender, ethnic, social, and cultural inequities. Narratives like the book of Esther, read with attention to the horrific events detailed throughout, can also invite us as readers and interpreters to wrestle with our understanding of the sacrality of human life and with whether the "sacred" texts that we have inherited and that we engage in our faith traditions and religious systems create and foster inclusion and a sense of community among all of humanity.

The story of Esther functions as a collective memory of Jews and details the horrors of sexual exploitation, colonialism, and cultural genocide in ways similar to how Africana people developed narratives to reflect on and critique experiences of sexual abuse, colonial domination, and cultural genocide. However, this story not only details the experiences of Jews but also of other racialized/ethnic groups, including Africana girls and women. Although the story is focused on the Jewish collective's struggles and interactions with imperial power, oppression, and exploitation, other ethnic groups are subjected to comparable struggles. This book, therefore, sheds light on how the ancient community and some contemporary readers and interpreters create social hierarchies that are used to suppress or erase the experiences and struggles of other ethnic groups that co-exist with the Jews in the story world. When this is recognized, it becomes evident that these narratively marginalized groups also struggle with access to power, sexual abuse, and other cultural oppressions.

I hope that the issues that I raise in this book prevent Africana and other minoritized cultural groups from absorbing further the violence of oppressive systems. I also hope that I have modeled and inspired ethically responsible and holistic interpretations of the biblical text that aid in our ability to identify sexual trafficking in ancient and contemporary contexts and that will galvanize us toward collective action that critiques gender hierarchies, patriarchy, colonialism, and dismantles sexual trafficking systems around the world.

One Night with the King? Another Consideration for Religious Leaders

The lyrics of a familiar song, "One Night with the King," originally sung by Aretha Franklin, and popularized in many Africana churches and communities by Prophetess Juanita Bynum, inadvertently normalize and promote sexualized violence against women – again, by ignoring the exploitative and abusive aspects of the narrative on which it is based. This is a result and consequence of appropriating, accepting, and internalizing dominant hegemonic biblical interpretations that mask exploitative ideologies and practices, especially concerning Africana people.[1]

In soulful melodious tones, both Franklin and Bynum lyrically assert that one night with the king can change "everything;" that one's destiny, from the desert to the palace, was chosen "for such a time as this" (Esther 4:14). It frames palace or harem life as a place for dreams to be transformed into realities.[2] Similar to some of the biblical interpreters I have engaged in this book, the lyricist frames "one night with the king" as an opportunity for economic and perhaps political advancement: as granting a female access to upward mobility, to making her "dreams to become realities" and changing the course of her life, forever, in a seemingly positive way. Unlike the biblical interpreters, however, the lyricist fails to specifically mention sex, let alone rape. The emphasis is on bettering the course of one's life. Indeed, one night with Ahasuerus changes the course of females' lives, but *not* in the romanticized or spiritualized way that it is framed and promoted in this song. Granted, Esther's life and livelihood are transformed and socially elevated. The virgin girls' lives and bodies, however, are marked by the trauma of violence at the hand of patriarchs, above all and most directly, by the king, and then discarded and suppressed in the narrative.

Related to this, hearers and interpreters of this song and – though less prominently – readers and commentators of the biblical narrative, conflate God and the king. In doing so, the king is framed as someone who cannot and should not be disobeyed or resisted, and the deity as someone like an imperial overlord, entitled to sexually exploit females. As I have discussed, similar blurring of religious (notably, divine) and sex trafficker imagery occurs in contemporary settings. One upshot of this is that authority is conferred from deity to abuser, and abusees are less able to distinguish between the deity and their pimp. Trust in biblical texts or religious institutions, too, may, in turn, come to be compromised, because biblical texts and those interpreting or preaching them are heard as alluding to, or echoing, exploitative notions.

The lyricist also conflates the traumatic experiences of sexual exploitation and threat of genocide with destiny and being chosen by the king, through incorporating the scriptural reference "for such a time as this." I do not believe that Franklin or Bynum would intentionally promote sexual trafficking. However, one legacy of appropriating dominant hegemonic biblical interpretation, is that some Africana readers/hearers fail to consider the interpretative impact and influence on Africana identity and culture. In the setting described in the biblical text, "one night with the king" can cause irrevocable and irreparable damage to Africana females' bodies, psyches, and future prospects. If we continue uncritically to disregard or to internalize cultural biases and read/interpret against our interests, as illustrated in the lyrics of this song and its role in worship experiences, we will silence or, worse, promote the sexual trafficking and abuse of our own collective.

As Africana peoples committed to liberation and justice, we must critique dominant interpretations of Esther 1–2 so that we can be life-giving and life-sustaining communities and support systems for one another. We, and our allies, must resist and rebuke interpretations of and ideologies in the sacred texts when these function to diminish Africana females' agency and lives. It is therefore essential for Africana biblical scholars, clergy, and lay persons to lead the way in transforming biblical interpretation through the implementation of intersectional polyvocal Africana biblical hermeneutics. Africana interpreters should foremost, recognize, center, and expand analysis to include African peoples in the text. In addition, we cannot select, or sound-bite, the verse in Esther 4 where Mordecai suggests Esther may have come to royal dignity, "for such a time as this." We cannot merely celebrate Esther's willingness or, decision to give in to pressure by Mordecai, to become a martyr for her people, without shedding light on the other women in the text and on the context, conditions, and actions that produced "a time as this."

In other words, in order to preach and teach on "such a time as this" or "one night with the king," interpreters, teachers, preachers, and readers must be attentive to the ancient context that produced this text and to intersecting race/ethnic, gender, class, and other aspects of identity that are at play in enactments of oppression and in the progression of the plot. Moreover, Africana interpreters should make connections between the sexualized violence perpetrated against the virgin girls and other enactments of violence against other social groups: not only in the book of Esther but throughout the Bible and history and up to the present.

For example, in the book of Esther, the sexual exploitation of Hadassah and possibly other Jewish virgin girls (outlined in Esther 2) is a problem that is connected to the gender hierarchy created in Esther 1, as well as to the threat of Jewish genocide in Esther 3, and the subsequent mass murders at the hand of the Jews in Esther 7–8. Similarly, the sexual trafficking of Africana girls and women is connected to racial and racist, alongside gender, hierarchies set up by colonizers, as well as to the enslavement and genocide of African peoples during the transatlantic slave trade, and to other manifestations of oppression and violence to Africana peoples. Issues of sexual exploitation, cultural genocide, and violence intersect as do the identities and oppressions of the cultural groups discussed in this book. In many instances, rape is a weapon of cultural genocide.

The book of Esther depicts a world in which the empire understands the worth of people in only utilitarian and consumptive terms. This portrayal may have contributed to the ways in which Africana people, Jews, and other minorities have been treated throughout history. Interpreters must gain the skills to recognize destructive ideologies before we can begin to address and challenge them. By focusing on Africana girls and women, I have identified and critiqued some of these damning ideologies and practices.

Moreover, this discourse necessitates acknowledgment and assessment of vulnerable geographies. Forced migration and exile are foundational experiences for African(a) girls and women both in the text and in contemporary contexts. Persian officials make strategic use of anxieties over gender and sexuality in order to legally facilitate forced migration and sexual trafficking, as they gather, abduct, and transport countless minoritized girls across national borders for the king's sexual pleasure. Specifically, girls in the text are taken from Indian and African locations. These geographies were central to the transatlantic slave trade as well. Thus, not only are the black and brown bodies of girls vulnerable to trafficking but my analysis also illuminates that the geographies themselves are vulnerable in sex trafficking economies.

In other words, there is a gendering of the geopolitical space. In the text, Persia is masculinized in its representation as the dominant geopolitical body that controls feminized and subordinate locales between India and Ethiopia. The colonized territories, meanwhile, are represented by feminized entities (namely, the virgin girls) who are taken and penetrated (that is, raped) by the Persian king. As the dominant geopolitical body and center, Persia controls the power relations in the international realm. Persian colonizers impact the gender, racial, and class climate of those under their rule. This is evident in the content and dispersal of their edicts, in who is hired or fired (e.g.,

Mordecai or Haman, Vashti or Esther) or executed (e.g., Haman, the eunuch would-be assassins), and in their control over who occupies what land or is displaced from their homelands. The Persian empire directs and dictates movement across national and international borders for sexual exploitation and the king's consumption. Persia controls transportation: of bodies and of imperial laws. The laws may be written in everyone's language and script, yet this is not for fostering diversity but for enforcing the authority of Persia alone. The power system is loaded: All power is located with the Persians and Medes. Similarly, during the colonial era, Europe represented the dominant geopolitical body, and its feminized colonies, too, were raped and coerced into benefiting Europe's trade networks and economies. Trade not only sustained the imperial system, but colonial authority also legitimated the constructions of gender that shaped Europe's trafficking enterprise, authorizing wide-scale sexual abuse against African diasporized females.

Closing Thoughts...

Re-reading the book of Esther with attention to intersectionality, polyvocality, and, specifically, with consideration of those with suppressed voices and identities has the potential to open readers and interpreters to increased knowledge and empathy. The horror of these experiences is brought into plain view when these lenses are applied to the text. For many readers, exposure to this trauma and horror triggers anger, outrage, grief, and even mistrust of those who have failed to identify and who continuously perpetuate, physically and narratively, injustices against Africana people. Collective memory enables us to better understand the past and present and, at the same time, galvanizes us to analyze the collective "us" through patterns of abuse and oppression perpetuated against us. In her essay, "The Site of Memory," Toni Morrison, reflecting on the historical, collective trauma of enslavement, cites two reasons for situating her work within the genres of autobiography and memoir: "This is my historical life – my singular, special example that is personal, but it also represents the race" and "I write this text to persuade other people – you, the reader, who is probably not black – that we are human beings worthy of God's grace and the immediate abandonment of slavery." Thus, the reflection upon and writing about Africana life, culture, histories, and memories becomes a means to relate our past and present experiences and, at the same time, to resist systemic exploitation, oppression, and other enactments of violence that endeavor to deny our humanity.

Socially located biblical interpretation provides scholars with opportunities to demonstrate leadership in galvanizing moments and movements for systemic change. Concretely, these types of interpretations facilitate social impact by challenging and changing rape cultures and other structural inequalities and social indignities that excessively impact Africana people. Coupled with social movements such as #SayHerName, the interpretation of Esther offered in this book is a timely response to the sexual abuse and silence around police brutality and the ruthlessness of those given the authority to "police" and violate Africana females' bodies and dignity. Like the #MeToo and #SayHerName movements, the stories that I have engaged in this book, alongside the stories raised by those movements, are powerful and demand that justice is actualized for those that have been targeted, traumatized, and often murdered by perpetrators of abuse.

If only we could join the chorus of #SayHerName supporters by lifting up the names of those Africana girls and women impacted by imperial violence in the book of Esther! We cannot because their names are irretrievable. But, as morally and ethically responsible biblical interpreters, we *can* bear witness to the plight of these girls and women whose names we will never know. We *can* stand with those impacted by sexual violence and exploitation throughout history and up to the present day, as we commit to read between the lines, behind the euphemisms, and through the silences and silencing in the biblical text and in narrated stories of Africana girls and women across time and space. In doing so, we may not redeem the biblical text, but we will redeem the stories and dignity of all the girls and women whose voices have too often been silenced.

Some stories cannot or should not be redeemed. Instead, these stories can and should teach readers about themselves and their roles in perpetuating oppressive ideologies and practices. Hopefully, sitting with the stories long enough and opening one's self up to different perspectives and interpretations of biblical narratives, will draw readers and interpreters to use their power, authority, and voices to be used to work toward eradicating oppression for all peoples and uplifting the stories of those whose voices and stories have been suppressed. I invite you to #SayHerName…. Hadassah! Vashti! …and to share the stories of the collective of Africana girls and women whose names we may never know. Their lives matter. Their voices matter. Use your power, agency, authority, and voice to challenge and eradicate violence and oppression.

Notes

1 As Randall C. Bailey notes, this type of careless interpretation presents a danger, because we are taught to ignore our "own cultural bias in interpreting" biblical texts. See Randall C Bailey, "The Danger of Ignoring One's Own Cultural Bias in Interpreting the Text," in *The Postcolonial Bible*, edited by R. S. Sugirtharajah (Sheffield: Sheffield Academic Press, 1998), 66–90.

2 "One Night with The King" (lyrics), accessed January 6, 2020, https://www.azlyrics.com/lyrics/arethafranklin/onenightwiththeking.html.

Index

For Product Safety Concerns and Information please contact our EU
representative GPSR@taylorandfrancis.com Taylor & Francis Verlag GmbH,
Kaufingerstraße 24, 80331 München, Germany

Printed and bound by CPI Group (UK) Ltd, Croydon, CR0 4YY
11/04/2025
01844010-0010